Financial Vision: The Classic Way to Create Wealth

A Practical Guide to the Art and Science of
Making Money and Managing Money

Financial Vision:
The Classic Way to Create Wealth

V. P. Sarin

MEGAGEM

Published by MergageM Sapience
www.megagem.org
gem@megagem.org

This publication is for educational purposes only. It is designed to provide accurate and authoritative information with regard to the subject matter covered. It should not be assumed that the methods and techniques presented in this publication will always be profitable or that they will not result in losses. Investing involves the risk of loss, as well as the potential for profit. Neither the publisher nor the author assumes any liability for any errors or omissions or for how this book or its contents are used or interpreted or for any consequences resulting directly or indirectly from the use of this book. It is not intended as a substitute for professional advice. Please consult an appropriate professional to address your specific needs.

ISBN-13: 978-8190889445
ISBN-10: 8190889443

Manufactured in the United States of America

Dedicated to those who step up to the challenges and become part of the solution

Contents

List of Illustrations

Preface

Money plays an important role in our lives, whether we have a lot or a little. But no school teaches us how to manage money. We learn it through trial and error. The problem with the unstructured learning is that many of us never understand how to deal with money. We rarely explore our relationship with money and try to understand whether money is a "means to an end" or an "end in itself."

Money can mean different things to different people. Some people see money as a means to an end and other people see money as an end in itself. Some rich people see money as an opportunity to help others and other rich people see their wealth as a tool to wield power. Sometimes the same person may see money differently in different circumstances Furthermore, the worth of money changes with change in situation. Besides, how can we define the worth of money that in itself defines worth, at least for lesser mortals?

Let me share a different perspective on wealth. I have many rich friends and relatives. Nearly all of them are getting richer, and many of them are multiplying their wealth year after year. But I consider my uncle Dr. Puri, a professor at a premier engineering institute, as the richest among them, who are certainly good at making money. My uncle's personal financial status is average. He does not own a big house or a great portfolio of investments. Why I consider him really wealthy when he hardly follows any moneymaking strategies discussed in this book?

Because he understands money. He knows it's true worth. He had a clear vision of future, which prompted him and his wife to invest their money and other resources on providing their three children the holistic upbringing and empowering them with all the important abilities including the ability to create wealth. Today their three investments individually have the potential to beat others not only in the moneymaking game, but also in the ultimate analysis of life, which is certainly a worthy achievement in itself. Their future vision may not have given them huge wealth, but they are really happy in the process of making others happy.

While financial vision is all about making money, it can never outsmart that sort of future vision. I know that admitting it can adversely impact the market potential of the book. But there is more to life than just money, and it is important to put the relative importance of money in perspective.

Moreover, this book does not claim to provide you a slot on the richest persons list or make you super rich next year. In fact, it is not for super people. It is for normal people who want to make the most of their financial resources. It is for people who have dreams and the resulting vision. It is not for negative people. For pessimistic people, tomorrow never arrives and yesterday keeps on replaying itself, albeit in slow motion. It intends to encourage positive people to optimally tap their financial potential. While the financial vision process encourages envisioning the financial future with the purpose of marrying the short term with the long term, it discourages the habit of 'wishful thinking' and aims at inculcating the habit of 'thoughtful wishes.'

What's more, financial vision is not just about making money. It is about validating your existence and fulfilling your desires. It is a way of reinventing and redefining your financial potential. It aims to empower you to harmonize your financial goals with your personal aspirations so that you can live your life as you wish. It provides a systematic and practical framework that seeks to enhance the psychological impact of the material, sometimes even at the expense of syntax because the objective is not to aim at an interesting read but to take care of your financial interests. The objective is to help you to rightly understand your financial vision, have conviction in it and take steps to make your financial dreams a reality. Simply put, it is intended to make you money conscious and empower you to realize your financial vision.

Keeping in mind that managing money is a skill that can be learned, let's envision the future. Let's discover your financial destiny.

V. P. Sarin

1. Money Matters: Making Sense of Money

Money is not the most important thing in our lives. But, it is required to enjoy most of the other important things in life. It is money that matters. Whether we like it or not, life revolves around money. Everyone wants money. It is money that makes the difference.

Unfortunately, today our existence is inevitably linked to money, and it is often considered as an important indicator of success. It is desirable to make money to provide for near and dear ones and the society. It is also good to make money to realize our cherished dreams. But if the sole purpose of making money is to get a slot in the richest persons list, it may not provide the much sought-after happiness or contentment. The desire to make money that stems from the acquisitive tendencies can be counterproductive.

Why money is so important for most human beings? While making sense of money, we can look at it in two basic ways. We need money for our needs, or we need it for our wants. Without sufficient sustenance, one cannot be happy and cannot imagine being happy in the future since the present circumstances color the way one envision the future. While a need is something that we have to have and a want is something we would like to have, individual needs and wants are somewhat fungible with subjective strings attached. An individual's need may be a distant dream i.e. a want for another person.

In distinguishing needs vs. wants, we may never get clarity as to whether need-based desires for money or want-based cravings for money are more prevalent in our society. Rationally the money ought to matter more to the really needy people. But it seems that it matters more to the people with never ending desires.

However, there are a few exceptions, who after reaching the pinnacle in the money making game, realize that money does not matter beyond a point. They seek a course correction with their philanthropic streaks to correct the money disparities between haves and have-nots. Be it Bill Gates or Warren Buffet or other members of the donors club, they cannot change the wide and persistent inequity between the haves and have-nots. While their humane actions are laudable, it has little impact on the social inequity, which is getting worse. We are becoming a society of haves and have-nots as the gap between the rich and poor is increasing.

But then, it is not the responsibility of the donors or the governments or any other entity to make you rich. Besides, our primary objective is to discuss how to make money and manage it optimally, and not to deliberate on what people do with their money. That is their prerogative. And why you want to make money is your prerogative. The theme of the book is to help all interested persons to create wealth irrespective of their financial standing. Further, it is easier to handle how to make money than to decide the right purposes of making money, especially if it involves the human desires rather than the human needs. The 'why' questions are invariably complex than the 'how' ones. Besides, they are often personal in nature and usually do not have standard answers. However, the future vision process mandates us to discuss some typical reasons for making money, which are essentially the need-based goals.

You cannot depend on others to fulfill your needs. It is your own responsibility to adequately provide for your family and realize your desires. You are accountable to yourself for creating wealth and managing it optimally. The second important aspect to keep in mind is that money is a good servant but a very bad master. So, you need to keep your sense of money in perspective. It is important to have the right perspective when it comes to making sense of money and managing it wisely to realize your dreams of a better future. The reason most people fail financially is not that they do not earn money but that they lose their sense of money. They do not know how to control and manage their money. Remember, controlling your money instead of letting your money control you give you a sense of empowerment and confidence, which is a prerequisite to create and preserve wealth. And that is the objective of the financial vision process.

The financial vision process intends to give you the information and the confidence you need to create wealth and realize your dreams. The financial vision process presumes that the ability to manage money is more important than having money. So, you can benefit from it whether you are rich and want to multiply your wealth or you first want to make money and manage it optimally to create wealth.

While making sense of money, never underestimate the role of control in money matters. Real financial freedom means you are in control of your money, not the other way round. Humans have a relationship with money that often goes beyond the financial freedom. Often their desire to make more and more money becomes the purpose of their life. Research confirms that above a certain level, money does not really matter; it does not add to happiness or satisfaction. Besides, money makes it difficult to identify true relationships. Yet, many of us like more and more money, and believe that it is easy to cope with the pressures of acquiring too much money. They believe, rightly or wrongly, that winning the money game is worth it. While some think that they can do a lot of social good with it in addition to securing their financial future, there are many others in the rat race who want to make money just for the sake of making money.

People often lose their sense of money in their moneymaking endeavors. There is no limit as to how much money they want. They do not really understand why they are greedy. In the moneymaking game, they often ignore the other players of life. They forget that life's other aspects are just as important as money. They forget that money matters when everything is in balance.

While recognizing that the unbridled quest for money is not good, the financial vision process encourages all positive people to be greedy. Your calculated, balanced greed is good for you, your family and the society as a whole. The positive people's money impacts humanity in a positive way. A high proportion of wealth with positive, caring people augurs well for the future of humanity. Yes, money can empower you to do a better job of making this world a better place to live. Your money can certainly make a difference to your life, and enable you to make a difference to the world in your own unique way if you really have the urge of 'doing good' and 'being good.' Having the right sense of money is important to make the difference that makes the real difference.

In our world, money is power. And powerful people can do what they want. Even the Bible says, "wine maketh merry: but money answereth all things" - Ecclesiastes 10:19. That is why it is good for the 'good guys' to have it and as much as possible. In short, the matters of money are obvious. If we could see.

Part 2

The Art of Managing Money

2.1 Financial Vision Process: An Overview

Most of us understand the importance of money in our lives. That is why we spend the bulk of our waking hours working for money. And we know that money management is vital to succeed in life. How we manage our money has a great deal to do with our personal happiness, our capacity to fulfill our financial needs, and to realize our financial aspirations. In spite of that, most of us pay negligible attention to our money management. We do not make sure that our money also works as hard as we work to earn it. While it is important how much money we make, but how much money our money makes for us is the key to create wealth.

People typically carry a false impression that money management is meant only for the rich. Money management is very important for every person whether one has enough money or meager resources. Rich people usually have a more discriminating understanding of how to use money to make more money. While the art of managing money helps the rich people to conserve and increase wealth, it provides an opportunity to the ordinary class to fulfill their financial needs as well as create wealth. So, the affluent and not so affluent classes equally need the personal financial management to make the best use of money and bring their dreams to fruition.

Personal Financial Planning vs. Financial Vision Process

Personal financial planning refers to the process of fulfilling financial goals through proper planning and management of finances. It helps you to find out where you are now, what you may need in the future and what you should do to meet your needs. It enables you to take a broad view of your financial situation and work out how to meet your financial needs. Personal financial planning enables you to draw a plan or strategy to realize your financial goals, such as children's education, home purchase and retirement planning. The personal financial planning approach is needs centered whereas financial vision process is vision-centered which aims to harmonize the financial vision with the financial needs in an attempt to make the most of resources.

So what is the financial vision process? The financial vision process is simply a matter of broadening the perspective from financial needs to financial vision wherein needs are also an integral part. The financial vision process is nothing but an advanced version of the personal financial planning. It strives to harmonize the financial perspectives with the personal aspirations. It is a systematic and all-inclusive approach to take care of the financial needs and desires whereas the personal financial planning is the chore of managing money just to look after the financial needs. The financial vision process does not undermine the significance of the financial planning rather supplements it by extending the compass, rationalizing the process and placing due emphasis on individual's lifetime interests. Simply put, it is simply a realistic assessment of your financial vision and the steps you must take to make your dreams a reality.

The financial vision process is the art and science of securing not just your financial needs but also make a sincere effort to realize your financial desires. It persuades you to conduct yourself in a manner where you are certain about not regretting your financial decisions later in life. It is the process to exploit your financial resources optimally to achieve your financial objectives as well as to control how each financial decision you make influences other areas of your life. So it is an organized and well-planned system of developing integrated strategies to convert your financial dreams into reality. A well-crafted financial vision in tandem with the sensible implementation strategies have the potential to serve as an antidote to the present day financial culture that encourages people to spend more, save little, and invest on an ad-hoc basis.

The personal financial planning is one of the most overused and much hyped catchphrases in the world of money management. But in practice it is too tricky to toe the line given that the basic makeup of the financial markets is not primarily conducive to take care of your overall financial interests. Financial markets are principally geared to serve the marketers' interests, which may be inconsistent with your interests. But if you rightly understand your financial vision, have conviction on it and all set to play a key role as a facilitator, everything else will follow the vision. The Personal financial vision process gives you a good idea of how to go a step further from just financial planning to manage your money more diligently to realize your dreams.

Benefits of Financial Vision Process

The financial vision process is essentially an ameliorated form of the personal financial planning. Because it stems from the financial planning, it offers all the benefits of personal financial planning such as inculcating better spending habits, providing improved lifestyle, taking care of current and future needs and accumulating wealth. Being more futuristic and individual-centric, the financial vision process accentuates all these benefits as well as brings in the following benefits.

1. The financial vision process gives a boost to 'the sense of wellbeing' by effectively countering financial uncertainties in addition to nurturing financial dreams.
2. It is dynamically aligned not just with your financial needs but also with your overall desires.
3. The process is very flexible and easily adaptable. The financial planning process is relatively rigid as compared to the financial vision process.
4. It gives requisite emphasis to human nature and provides for a mechanism to mitigate financial setbacks due to our weak or vulnerable areas, i.e., our Achilles' heels that we all have.
5. Clear demarcation of the process in procedural, protective and promising segments makes the steering efficient and the process result-oriented.
6. The bidirectional nature of this process ensures better monitoring of the financial interests and timely adjustments to capitalize on contemporary opportunities.
7. People, who routinely see in their mind's eye their financial dreams, tend to put greater efforts for fulfilling their vision resulting in better success rate.

8. The self-directing approach of this process helps you to clarify aspirations in all areas of life and to design an appropriate financial strategy to support those aspirations.
9. This empowers you to create an enduring financial success because your vision provides the conviction to do what really matters to you.
10. Participating in the process makes one progressively more adept at dealing with financial ups and downs in a dispassionate manner thereby minimizing the negative impact on other aspects of life.
11. It anticipates changes all along and is flexible enough to adapt to changes to facilitate successful transitions. It empowers you to develop a knack of how to perceive and respond to changes so as to optimize your money management endeavors.
12. It keeps all-important financial goals in balance and harmony, which enables you to aptly prioritize to make sure that you are not consumed by some goals leading to the omission of others.
13. It puts your interests on the front burner instead of sellers' business.
14. It extends perspective from just narrow financial goals to the broader life-centric issues.

It takes a little dose of wisdom and the right processes to make your money work harder for you. The financial vision process helps you to do just that to transform your financial dreams into reality. This process acts as an efficient and dependable roadmap to flourish in the ultimate analysis of lifetime money management. This process addresses your entire financial picture and allows you to create your own financial strategies to provide direction and meaning to your financial endeavors. The financial vision process not only helps you even out the vicissitudes on your journey to a secure financial future, but also suggests a sustainable long-term path to create wealth along the way.

The financial vision process lays out a simple structure for a person interested in improving her/his financial health perpetually. This process comprises of two main phases namely — defining phase and execution phase. Defining phase is to help you establish the roadmap i.e. Financial Vision Statement, which covers your financial needs as well as desires. The next phase i.e. Execution Phase assists you to be in control and on the right track on the road to realizing your financial vision.

Devising Financial Vision

The saying, "If you do not know where you are going, you will end up somewhere else" implies here that not knowing your vision well is the surest way to go away from it. It is very true that our aspirations play a big role in our success, especially financial success. Defining our financial vision is all about identifying our financial needs and exploring our financial aspirations. Simply put, it makes us realistically aware of our truly preferred financial objectives.

The financial wellbeing is considered crucial to the overall wellbeing for both individuals and organizations. The financial vision statement is often regarded as the central guiding light to achieve the objectives of the organization. Likewise, individuals are also increasingly adapting the various money management tools and techniques to improve their financial status. Because finance is the all-important lifeline for survival and growth, the financial vision becomes imperative for individuals and legal entities alike. But surprisingly, our experience reveals that the financial vision statements are more effective and as such have better success rate in the personal context than in the organizations. This is truer particularly for well-qualified professionals. This is primarily because individuals purposely contribute in the making of their own financial vision statements and have a final word as to what should be the right vision statement to ensure a gratifying future. So, big organizations as well as small investors can take advantage of this strategic tool to make the best use of scarce resources to exploit viable opportunities aimed at creating wealth.

The financial vision statement provides a holistic view of an individual's financial interests. By providing a central reference point, it helps you to stay focused on your objectives since you can manage it all from one statement. Having a clear vision of your goals could be of great help when you take the important financial decisions. It imparts momentum to your financial endeavors as you can clearly see the light at the end of the tunnel. In order to create a pragmatic financial vision that aligns the long-term vision with the short-term objectives, it is necessary to undertake the following steps.

Brainstorming

The first step in devising your financial vision is a broad brainstorming exercise wherein you just have to scribble down whatever financial issues cross your mind. You may do well by exploring your financial needs as well as envisioning your financial desires. Further, you may like to segregate your needs & desires in short, intermediate and long-term categories. At this stage, you are not supposed to discard any idea, need, desire, dream, or even daydream by using viability filter or any other line of reasoning. You ought to write down even the financial goals, which you are diligently pursuing and are on the right track. Writing is important here as it extracts, enlightens and elucidates ideas, and combines the conscious with the subconscious mind. Every now and then, each of us indulges in a placid form of brainstorming, though we may not be fully aware of this activity of the subconscious mind. This formal exercise is intended to capture the big picture of what you consciously or subconsciously expect from your financial vision. So, this exercise needs to be done at least twice on different days in order to minimize the influence of temperamental swings in envisioning the financial wish list. This will go a long way in exploring the potentially satisfying elements to crate a financial vision that coalesces well with your future vision.

Examining

Next, you need to critically examine the outcome of your brainstorming exercise that is your wish list. Not everyone will have the same wish list, even though such lists often have some common goals. Your wish list is based on your own ideas, and it is not imposed on you by someone else. It is a personal transcript which cannot be judged vis-à-vis any standard wish list. So, you have to objectively revisit your wish list to check whether your list requires some changes. Remember, dealing intelligently with your financial aspirations is an art, which could confer immense practical and financial benefits.

Examining your financial goals involves analysis and synthesis. Here analysis implies dissecting and synthesis implies coalescing. Examining your financial desires is the crucial part of the entire financial vision process because you have several goals to choose from where each goal has its positive and negative features. So it becomes imperative on your part to examine this list rationally to prune it, as each goal requires resources to achieve. Resources, in terms of money, time and efforts are always limited and you should explore only those options where payback is optimum. This is all the more important since negative filters are usually curbed at the brainstorming stage with a view to encourage free flow of ideas. So, at this stage you need to ask yourself the following questions because a successful financial vision statement is based on seeking the right answers to the right questions.

- ✓ Is this goal important to my family & me?
- ✓ What are the benefits of reaching this goal?
- ✓ Is this goal believable, measurable, attainable, and desirable?
- ✓ What resources do I need to accomplish the goal?
- ✓ Do I clearly understand the impact of this financial goal on other financial issues?
- ✓ What are the obstacles that could prevent me from achieving this goal?
- ✓ Do I have a plan and wherewithal to overcome the anticipated obstacles?
- ✓ Whether this goal is life centered and in harmony with my values and priorities.
- ✓ Am I willing to pay the price to realize this goal?
- ✓ Am I realistic about this goal?

Answering the above questions will help you prioritize your goals by selecting what works best for you. By examining your values, desires, financial perspectives and preferred outcomes as they relate to your financial needs and priorities, you can identify the elements of your financial vision, which relate in a dynamic way with your future vision. Bear in mind that no one can achieve every financial dream and so while discarding or deferring some goals, suppress the urge to cling to your cherished but unviable goals. Formulating your financial vision is a dynamic process, which will provide you many opportunities to revisit what is left. Remember, you have a better chance of getting what matters most to you by focusing your efforts to a select few.

Converting to Specific Objectives

After expanding and narrowing down your financial wish list, the next step is to put together your financial vision statement that will be a tentative blueprint to secure your financial future. It is important to put down in black and white your chosen financial goals along with justifications to have a clear picture of what you expect from your financial vision process. So you should write down specific, measurable, attainable, sensible, and time bound objectives on the way to map out suitable strategies to turn your vision into reality. You should decide on a definite time frame to clarify whether your objectives are short term or long term. Clear and precise objectives will provide purpose, focus and direction to the financial vision process. You get a good head start towards successful money management when you have a clear understanding of your objectives as well as underlying reasons. While firming up your financial objectives, you have to accord priority to a few that can help you feel financially secure and satisfied. So after identifying your goals, you should prioritize them according to their importance in your life.

A vision statement cannot be written overnight. It takes time, as you may have to rewrite it several times before you feel at home with it. Please do not seek shortcuts because the exercise of defining your financial vision is as important as the vision statement. Keep in mind that we reflexively spend a lot of time on similar mental exercises owing to our dabbling nature, though we may not realize it per se. Here you need to devote a little extra time to devise your formal financial vision in a structured way in order to put it into the right perspective, thus making it more effective and executable.

Since financial vision process is a dynamic and bidirectional process, your vision statement is not supposed to be cast in stone. You will always get many opportunities to choose along the way. The above steps are the general guidelines in creating your first formal financial vision statement. Since each individual and his/her circumstances are unique, these steps may have to be supplemented in the light of your particular situation.

At this stage, the financial vision statement ought to be a broad-brush perspective plan, to be reviewed and duly modified at every stage in the financial vision process, and as such should not to be considered a sacrosanct plan. Reviewing the financial vision is an ongoing process and you need to revisit it at predetermined intervals as well as whenever there is any significant change in the circumstances having an impact on your finances. In today's overly complex and ever-changing world, it is desirable to adapt a flexible approach to your financial vision process since economy, market dynamics, tax laws, your career vision and other personal factors will all fluctuate and require frequent adjustments to your financial vision. In addition, your financial priorities invariably change as you age, so you should preferably reexamine your financial needs and desires at least every three years.

Executing Financial Vision

There is an old adage, "a roadmap will get you to the foot of the mountain, but perseverance will make you climb it." Financial vision statement can open the doors to financial success, but only proactive and persistent approach can keep them open. The execution phase involves looking for effective ways to make the connection between aspirations and realization. The aim is to provide a pragmatic and doable model to turn the vision into reality.

In today's cutthroat existence, all of us are busy with our own matters. So we tend to procrastinate, particularly new endeavors, invariably discounting the significance of the task and often disregarding the probable consequences in our life. Moreover, the money management is a very involved process with little room for errors, and as such, necessitates commitment and perseverance to derive material benefits from the process. Therefore, we need to keep it all-inclusive yet simple exercise because a pointlessly complex exercise is vulnerable to fritter away our efforts on secondary issues wherein effort to reward proportion may not compare favorably. Further, in order to provide some flexibility to maneuver as the situation demands, we have divided the process in three segments namely procedural, protective, and promising elements. Notwithstanding this segmentation, most of the elements are meant to reinforce each other and to build on each other.

Procedural Elements

The purpose of this step is to empower you to continually monitor your financial health and make sure that your money management is on the right track. It is similar to your routine health checkups except that in this case time is your ally not like physical health where time is destined to play a negative role in the future. These elements let you find out where you are and how you are moving. They provide direction and control to your money management efforts and inculcate the requisite discipline for achieving your financial vision. They guide you to evolve a personal mechanism to monitor the progress of your financial initiatives. The procedural aspects along with the financial vision statement make a perfect combination of roadmap with compass, exemplifying the clear-cut way forward to realize your goals.

Procedural elements can be broadly classified into three elements namely– Getting Organized, Evaluating Financial Health and Improving Financial Fitness. These are much more than mere procedures. These are specifically designed to ensure that best practices are applied to the money management for maximum returns and optimum wealth creation. Considering the significance of these elements, we shall discuss these in detail in the succeeding chapters wherein you will appreciate how these are applied to real life situations.

Protective Elements

The basic makeup of the financial vision process often misled people to think about money management as an entirely and inherently personal issue, but actually many external factors do play a part in managing money effectively. These external factors like taxes, insurance, miscellaneous family needs and future concerns invariably clamor for precedence over financial desires, which incidentally are the sought-after part of the vision statement. The future vision process appreciates that there is nothing wrong in assigning priority to the protective elements over the promising goals. But restricting your financial universe to merely supporting subsistence often becomes a stumbling block in unleashing your true financial potential. And that should be guarded against. Nevertheless, the protective elements deserve precedence since they are essential to provide a favorable ambiance for other spheres of life including the promising goals to flourish.

Our experience reveals that most of us are well versed with the protective elements, as they invariably appear to be obligatory while treading the path of day-to-day money management. Often rigors of daily routine make them more compelling than other financial elements. But, even protective elements are dissimilar for each individual. Moreover, some of these elements are constantly changing shape, especially those impacted by taxes, economic conditions, market dynamics, career and family concerns. Therefore, unique circumstances of each individual necessitate tailor made solutions to take care of her/his protective elements i.e. basic financial requirements. In view of this, it may be counter productive to suggest standard solutions in this category. Yet, we cautiously take up some of the key protective elements to address the general financial concerns as well as enable you to complete the big picture of the financial vision process.

Insurance Analysis

Insurance is an important risk management mechanism that allows common people to avail financial protection and share losses. Insurance cover is meant to protect financial interest in something such as life, disability, health, home and vehicle. Pensively appraising insurance needs is the first and foremost part of the protective elements. Insurance helps you to safeguard the people and things that matter most to you and to assure you that your family is protected against unforeseen events. It is important to have an adequate insurance cover to bring down risks in the financial vision process. In short, insurance analysis entails recognizing what risks you are exposed to and deciding how to control those risks.

The basic purpose of life insurance is to safeguard the financial interests of the near and dear ones in case of unforeseen circumstances. It is meant to replace the income in order to provide funds to the loved ones to carry on with a reasonable lifestyle. So it provides the peace of mind to you and safety net to your family members. Life insurance covers can be broadly classified in two categories. Term policies are just pure protection cover and offer benefit for the agreed period in case of death. Cash-value or whole life insurance provides death benefit as well as an investment component. Accumulated cash-value components can be used like any other saving. Individual's needs determine how much insurance cover one should take. As a rule of thumb, people should make sure that their assets including insurance cover are not less than ten times their net annual income.

The next important insurance cover is health insurance wherein payment is dependant on the insured incurring medical expenses or losing income because of health problems. Health insurance covers expenses such as hospitalization, doctor's fees, medicines and other illness related expenses. Disability insurance even provides for the lost income when unfitness prevents the person from normal working.

The next step in the risk appraisal context is to evaluate the insurance needs of assets against losses caused by natural and man-made perils such as theft, fire, floods and other calamities. Relevant assets for insurance include home, vehicles, equipments, furniture & fixtures, jewellery, and other valuable personal assets. House insurance policy including household items is particularly important to instill a sense of security. People work hard, save systematically and plan carefully to purchase a house, but often forget or ignore to insure it. Remember, house is generally the major material asset, which gives shelter as well as act as an emotional lynchpin.

Insurance analysis may not be very important for the rich people with well-diversified assets portfolio, as they can depend on their capital reserves for unforeseen eventualities. But it is imperative for people who have not saved enough to take care of contingencies. Adequate life and health insurance cover should be a priority for all such people.

Current Needs & Future Goals

This protective element is primarily meant to provide for the necessities of the life – present as well as future. Current needs simply refer to maintaining the reasonable standard of living and fulfilling all necessities in the day-to-day life. After providing for all the essentials, we engage in the 'spending vs. saving' debate: to spend on the current desires or to save for the future needs. The 'spending vs. saving' debate or dilemma is as old as civilization. This debate has no concrete answers, as the outcome cannot be all out supportive of either spending or savings. It is not an all or nothing matter. It is essentially a matter of determining share of savings out of the current income that too depending on the prevailing circumstances of the person concerned. So this seemingly simple but dynamic protective element demands hands on approach to strike just the right balance between current needs and future objectives. At the same time, one should bear in mind that no one could have everything she/he wants. So it is essentially a question of making the most of your resources by judicious choices. Even super-rich have to choose what they really want, as they cannot get all they yearn for. In order to achieve an optimum balance, we need to adopt the personal budget to forecast and monitor our spending so as to earmark a reasonable share for our future needs. In chapter titled Improving Your Financial Health, we will take up these aspects thoroughly with illustrations.

Tax Planning

It is important to understand how taxes affect your finances in order to implement an effective tax planning strategy to minimize taxes. Tax evasion or tax planning can reduce the impact of taxes on our income. The tax evasion is not only against the law, but also morally incorrect. While tax evasion is clearly deplorable, even tax avoidance by resorting to loopholes in the law should also be questioned. Avoiding tax using legal ambiguities may not be wrong in terms of the letter of the law, but it ought to satisfy our scruples. However, tax management by using allowable benefits is desirable not just to maximize post tax income but also to serve the larger purpose for which these benefits are intended. Tax planning is an entitled and smart way of managing taxes within the permissible stipulations of the relevant authorities.

We are well aware that the money management is a personalized exercise. Tax planning makes it somewhat more dynamic because applicable provisos vary not from place to place, but also keep on changing from time to time. Frequent changes in tax laws and rules influence tax consequences. So, we need to understand the intricacies and implications of taxation laws and benefits to make sure that we are not gratuitously losing substantial part of our income to taxes.

We can maximize post tax income by implementing several strategies such as investing in tax shelters, maximizing deductions, availing exemptions on retirement/pension plans, and the like. We should not single-mindedly consider reducing taxes; rather, we should examine all the options to select the one that optimizes our taxes and is in line with our financial needs. Preferably, our tax decisions should be influenced by holistic tax planning within the framework of our overall financial vision process. It is desirable to seek professional advice on the special issues involved in our tax planning whenever we find it difficult to take up this on our own.

Retirement Planning

Retirement is certain, but the time of retirement is uncertain, especially for the dynamic people. Traditionally, retirement planning entailed arranging finances for the post retirement period. In future, this approach may not be adequate given that ever-increasing longevity is continually leading to expanding proportion of seniors in the total population. Vision revision process emphasize more on lever-aging age to make the most of experience during golden years rather than just planning finances for later years. Notwithstanding all this, the importance of planning finances for the post retirement period cannot be undermined. And it cannot be denied that old age brings with it many health problems, which usually require increased expenses. Financial planning for later years involves estimating expenses during retirement and arranging sufficient funds to meet these expenses. When this process is undertaken at an early age, the power of compounding progressively adds to the retirement kitty because of the concept of time value of money.

Retirement planning is a multifaceted and significant aspect of the financial vision process bearing in mind ever-increasing number of years one has to spend in retirement. This necessitates a comprehensive retirement plan in order to make the most of the last one-third lifespan. In general, professionals are more prone to defer their future planning even though they are fully aware of unequivocal advantages it offers. Considering the importance of getting the best from golden years, all these issues are comprehensively discussed in the last part of the book

Estate planning

People spend their lifetime in assiduously planning how to create and conserve wealth, but tend to ignore the fact that they cannot continue to do so forever. Understandably, it may be overwhelming for some to plan for such an eventuality. But it is important to make sure that your loved ones' future is by your choice, and not by chance. An estate comprises of things you own and estate planning deals with passing it on to the heirs in an easy, efficient and empathetic way. Estate planning is the process of arranging transfer of assets to the near and dear ones according to the wishes and discretion of the individual. This definition implies that a person has to draw on his discretion in respect of the three main areas: Assets Planning, People Planning and Transfer Planning.

Assets Planning involves determining the present status of your estate i.e. assets minus liabilities.

This is also known as personal financial status, which is discussed in detail in the chapter 'Evaluating Your Financial Health.' The personal financial status is the starting point to plan inheritance effectively. The process of making the personal financial status will take care of the necessary aspects of the assets planning in the context of the estate planning.

People Planning requires anticipation of the needs of the heirs or beneficiaries. It is particularly important for people who have dependant kindred. It primarily involves deciding beneficiaries as well as how assets are to be distributed among them. People Planning also covers succession planning for the business enterprises, trusts, etc.

Transfer Planning aspects deal with the modus operandi of distribution and disposition of estate to the beneficiaries. Here are some of the factors to be deliberated to ensure trouble-free transfer.

➤ To decide the transfer methods, i.e., transfer by will, through trust, life insurance benefits, annuities, etc. after the death

➤ To provide for adequate liquidity to meet the estate obligations and transfer costs

➤ To decide on the executor, attorney and other persons responsible for transfer of the assets

➤ To estimate estate tax liability and make provision for the same

➤ To decide on a simple and cost effective implementation process

➤ To decide the beneficiary for the residual estate after meeting all the specific bequests

People often procrastinate to plan their estate. Estate planning is an intricate and protracted process, which involves facing the certainty of death. Reluctance to estate planning is understandable, but the potential benefits make it a mandatory exercise. Here are some of the benefits.

✓ It assures distribution of assets as per individual's wishes.

✓ It averts potential problems and family conflicts.

✓ It offers trouble-free sharing that minimizes expenses and taxes.

✓ It makes the sharing process emotionally easier.

✓ It minimizes or eliminates the legal hassles.

✓ It ensures cost-effective continuity of the business enterprises, trusts, etc.

Since all the financial elements are interlinked, they are important for realizing our financial vision. Occasionally we may have to accord relative priorities to some of these. But some of the protective elements often clamor for more than appropriate attention possibly owing to our weaknesses and/or external influences. We have to establish the right balance to avert imbalances in our approach. 'What if' analysis enables us to do this as well as put other elements in proper perspective to determine their right place in the urgent-important status.

Promising Elements

Primary concern of all the creatures is to fulfill their life's necessities. Most of the human beings are no different and perceive merely life's basic needs as the first and foremost as well as the ultimate concern. A recent United Nations study confirms that the world's richest 2% own more than half of global wealth while half the world's population own just 1%. Unfortunately, very few go beyond the necessities and go all-out to create wealth so as to empower themselves to take good care of their near and dear ones. Creating wealth also enables individuals to contribute to the economy as well as society even supposing they do not directly indulge in philanthropy.

The promising elements are particularly intended for people who work hard to make money. With a little extra effort, they can make sure that their money also works harder to fulfill their financial aspirations. In the wealth creation game plan, it is more important how you can multiply your money than how much money you make. This is clearly demonstrated by the majority of first generation high net worth individuals who have created most of their wealth using prudent and balanced investment strategies. The wealth created by most of these individuals on their investments clearly surpasses their entire career's earnings.

Promising elements are the most complex yet dynamic part of the financial vision process. They entail a high risk-reward dimension, which calls for the right mix of optimism and pessimism. Optimists who invariably expect staggering returns are likely to be ill prepared for the economic downturns and market declines. On the other hand, pessimists who tread the most cautious path in investing may not be able to reap the benefits of wealth creation opportunities. While it may be prudent to tread cautiously amidst euphoria, it may be equally prudent to take calculated bold steps amidst dysphoria to capitalize on opportunities. This means you have to take a realistic view of the situation. But then, most of the optimists and pessimists regard themselves realistic. Therefore, you need to take a holistic view in this wealth creation game wherein promising elements empower you to arrive at the right mix of investments considering your unique profile.

Promising elements are more to do with the art of making money from money that is essentially investment planning. Small investors generally prefer conservative approach to investing and this explains why a large number of investors are smitten with the mutual funds of all types. But lately more and more individual investors are venturing into all kinds of investments expecting their cut in the ever-increasing prosperity. In view of the significance of the wealth creation issues and overwhelming interest shown by the middle class in the promising goals, these elements justify an exhaustive examination that we shall do in the next part of the book.

The financial vision process may be a little tricky to understand initially but it is very easy to implement. It appears to be difficult, as it demands unemotional and rational approach to your financial decisions just to fulfill your endearing and enduring desires. Once you start using this process diligently, it will progressively become an easy, enjoyable and rewarding experience.

2.2 Getting Organized for Money Makeover

We spend most of our waking hours making money, and the rest expending it. While money plays a central role in our lives, yet we rarely devote any time to organize our financial records. More often than not, we belong to the accumulate-and-procrastinate school of personal record keeping. Many of us keep our financial records in a hodgepodge manner. We randomly note down our financial transactions even though we know it is always better for our financial health to do the same in a well thought-out and organized way.

Simple organization of financial records is not only time-efficient but also much easier than rummaging through a cluttered mess. Well-ordered financial records can put an end to searching for the lost records in the heaps of old and new documents and can help us bring order out of chaos. It also helps us save time and money while keeping us serene to focus on the more important decision-making aspects of money management.

While most of us are well acquainted with the reliable record keeping practices, procrastination often comes in the way of ordered personal records. This often set in motion a chain reaction whereby this seemingly small problem slowly but surely becomes acute before we know it. This not only muddle up the important financial documents but as well get in the way of efficient money management. Many well-qualified people are not adept at managing their personal finances primarily because of this reason. Experts pinpoint this factor as the principal reason why so many successful people trail behind others in the ultimate analysis of wealth creation. While successful professionals are generally good at analyzing and interpreting information, which are essential prerequisites for managing money, they often fail to get the structured information on their finances to carry on.

Hypothesizing if you do not get anything from this book; just take charge of your record keeping system and have a second look even if you consider it good enough. This will definitely recompense you many times your efforts. You can expect rich dividends in the long-term as well as short-term. Remember that you can always improve on your system; besides, the time spent in this exercise has the potential to give you many new insights on your financial affairs.

To substantiate our contention, we would like to recount that earlier we used to consider our standard record-keeping format as comprehensive, efficient and adaptable enough to cope with the needs of most of our clients. Our complacency never allowed us to genuinely review the basic framework to pursue probable improvements. While graduating to the financial vision process at the turn of 21st century, we had to streamline it to make it more amenable to the analytical needs obligated by the proposed process. And the modification of our classification to align it appositely with the new process created the new clear-cut and practical labeling method. Now we realize that our new system still provides all the benefits of the earlier version, and it is very simple to operate as well as facilitates logical thinking. This prompted us to follow the mandate 'Keep it simple, relevant and interesting' while addressing the procedural elements. We suggest the same to you to reap the optimum benefits of the ongoing review and updating process in your financial endeavors.

Even though most of you are well aware of the benefits of a simple, systematic and workable record keeping system, we shall now sum up the advantages to overemphasize this element because it is not just a question of the benefits rather it is central to the financial progress.

- ✓ It saves time, money and efforts. Saved resources can be better exploited to make intelligent use of the data to improve our financial health.
- ✓ It ensures the right information in the right place, in the right form, and in reasonable details to meet our needs.
- ✓ It makes money management easier and allows us to efficiently work on the protective and promising elements, which are the keys to unlock our financial vision.
- ✓ The process of organizing records is a good way to reacquaint ourselves with some of the neglected but

important areas of our financial affairs. Secondly, it enables us to periodically discard the redundant records.

✓ In case of health or other emergencies, it eases the stress and enables other family members to easily retrieve information and other financial documents.

✓ It allows us to firm up our stand while dealing with institutions, such as banks, insurance companies and tax authorities.

✓ It makes us responsive to our financial health, and that empowers us to control unfavorable situations efficiently and effectively to minimize or avoid the losses as well as work towards maximizing potential gains.

✓ We are better equipped to recognize problems that require attention even in other areas of life, and as such can optimize outcomes in other spheres.

✓ It empowers us to devise our financial strategies on the basis of relevant data and information, as against ad-hoc financial decisions.

✓ A well-structured system eases the pressure of making financial statements and keeping these up-to-date.

✓ Structured information enables us to make the most of potential opportunities in a coolheaded manner.

Components of the Personal Record Keeping System

We will now take up the essential components of a reliable record keeping system to make the most of our financial endeavors. Establishing a formal record keeping system consists of broadly three steps: Organizing, Safe Keeping, and Critiquing.

Organizing

The first step in the process of evaluating your financial health is to create a mechanism to organize all your financial records. Only a systematic yet simple scheme for keeping track of important records can make it easier to manage complex financial issues productively. User-friendliness is imperative to ensure the right analysis and continuity in the personal record keeping. The most of the record-keeping systems available in the market are either too complicated or too generalized to serve the requirements of the majority of people. So we are essentially seeking a system that is adaptable enough to conform to our requirements as well as support our existing and new moneymaking endeavors without increasing the complexity of the personal record keeping.

We are well aware that overall financial health depends on many factors, ranging from the various protective elements to the envisioned promising elements. Many financial elements are interconnected and/or interdependent on other elements. This calls for a complex and comprehensive structure to bring about total perfection in the procedural aspects. However, our intention is not to seek theoretical perfection in the procedural elements. Rather we would opt for a pragmatic approach in the indexing structure to initiate a simple and clear-cut working system that helps us to actualize our financial vision conveniently. The simplicity and added functionality of the proposed structure will enable us to improve the management of protective and promising elements, which actually matter in the ultimate analysis.

Bearing this in mind, I suggest the following basic groupings to label all your financial records. This coding structure is essentially designed to simplify the intricate financial issues.

Personal Coding Structure

Group	Range	Description
1	1.1 to 1.9	Assets/ Investments
2	2.1 to 2.9	Liabilities
I	I.1 to I.9	Income (Revenue income)
E	E.A to E.Z	Expenses (Revenue expenses)
3	3.1 to 3.9	Income (Capital income)
4	4.1 to 4.9	Banks/ Budget & Cash flow
5	5.1 to 5.9	Personal
6	6.1 to 6.9	Insurance Documents
7	7.1 to 7.9	Tax Related Papers
8	8.1 to 8.9	Retirement Planning
9	9.1 to 9.9	Estate Planning
0	0.1 to 0.9	Miscellaneous

This concept of coding records is actually very simple. To demonstrate how easy it is to apply codes to the financial documents, let us walk through a sample filing scheme for the assets of Ms. S.Ample.

Personal Records - Sample Filing Scheme

Code	File Description	Comments
1	**ASSETS**	
1.1	**Liquid Financial Assets:-**	
1.11	Cash	Notional file
1.12	Bank Balances	City Bank, Ab Bank
1.13	Fixed Return Instruments	Cash equivalent=…,
……	……	
1.19	Miscellaneous	Notional file
1.2	**Other Fin. Investments:-**	
1.21	Equity	
1.22	Bonds	
1.23	Commodities	
1.24	Mutual Funds	Equity=.., Bonds=..,
1.25	Present value of Insurance	Copy in file 5.1(Ins.)
……	……	
1.29	Miscellaneous	
1.3	**Physical Assets:-**	
1.31	Home	Copy in file5.1(pers)
1.32	Real Estate Investments	
1.33	Precious Metals	Gold, Silver, …
1.34	Artworks	
……	……	
1.39	Miscellaneous	
1.4	**Personal Assets:-**	
1.41	Vehicles	Copy in file5.1(pers)
1.42		
1.43	Jewelry/ Precious Items	
1.44	Artwork	
……	……	
1.49	Miscellaneous	cont.>>

Code	File Description	Comments
1.9	**Other Assets:-**	
1.91	Business	
.....	.....	
1.99	Miscellaneous	
1.0	**Deferred Assets**	
1.01	Pension/Retirm. Plans worth	Copy in file 8.1 (ret.)
1.02	Royalty on Books	
.....	......	
1.09	Miscellaneous	

While discussing other elements of the financial vision process, we will elaborate the various attributes of this coding scheme. Subsequent chapters will take up more examples to familiarize you with the setting up of the coding scheme, which makes it easy to organize records as well as generate personal financial statements quickly. You will observe that this seemingly simple coding structure is versatile enough and can be suitably modified to suit your requirements. However, incase of any difficulty you may consult your financial advisor or contact us.

Safe Keeping

Before we proceed to examine maintenance aspects of a well-organized record keeping system, it is advisable to put in place a simple and hard-wearing filing system to store your financial records. An efficient filing system needs to support a pertinent coding structure to derive full benefits of an integrated money management process. You should set up a filing system that is simple, efficient, and assist in the analytical decision-making. With this framework, one can seamlessly rummage into even the mountain of financial data and derive valuable insights from the information to spearhead the wealth creation quest.

You have to keep in mind that some financial records need to be reflected in more than one category. For instance, insurance premium on your personal car has to be depicted in insurance, budgets, expense categories as well as a part of assets category in the relevant asset file. This you can do by keeping photocopies in the relevant files with cross references. Alternatively, you may keep the document in the main category and appropriately annotate other relevant files.

A basic safekeeping system should have the following main groupings:

A deposit box

The objective of the deposit box is to keep all very important papers (VIP's) such as personal, legal, leases, contracts, home ownership, other important titles, investments, insurance, wills and the like. You should also keep a photocopy of all these VIP's in your working folder kept at home as well as appropriately annotate in the proxy file meant for contingencies such as medical emergencies.

A working folder kept at home

This is the most functional category that is intended for keeping all the current records, important as well as trivial. This folder must be conveniently located and ensure ease of use because it is designed for more than 90% of the financial records. All records relating to the current year as well as previous year are normally kept in this group. Busy people prefer to accumulate all incoming papers in one assorted file and organize them weekly or monthly in the appropriate files.

A dormant folder kept at home or in storeroom

As the name suggests this folder contains all superfluous records, which may be required in future to substantiate tax returns, capital gains/losses, old contracts, etc. People like to first shift two/three years old important records to this folder annually and keep them in the specially created file for that particular year to facilitate future retrieval and discarding process. It is also a good practice to dump unneeded papers first in a period file in the inactive folder to reduce the burden of working folder. These period files can be easily discarded later on.

A proxy file

The purpose of proxy file is to enable your nominated person to take charge of your financial affairs in case of health or any other emergency. It also serves as a backup arrangement for you.

The proxy file contains an index, copies of important documents and a brief guide to the financial issues.

Critiquing

As our life grows more and more complex, we accumulate large numbers of financial papers. Yet many of us hardly ever bother to critically review our cumulative collection of important or unneeded documents. This not just has the potential to apply the brakes on our financial progress, but can also deprive us an opportunity to reacquaint ourselves with some of the overlooked parts of our money management. Critiquing allows us to scrutinize our recordkeeping system for probable improvements, and check the accumulated records to find out the ways to strengthen the safekeeping system. This also enables us to keep what we need and toss the rest.

A good critiquing routine is an indispensable component of a robust record keeping system. An efficient and functional system calls for periodical review as well as removal of unneeded records to avert pointless bulging of your folders. You have to establish the financial housecleaning guidelines to keep what you need and toss the rest. If you are not sure how long to retain financial records, you may seek the advice of relevant authorities or ask your personal financial advisor.

If you tend to procrastinate periodic reviewing of your records, you have not adapted the sound record-keeping habits. Remember, this seemingly insignificant task can derail your record-keeping system. At least once a year you should go through all your records and discard everything that is no longer needed.

The art of managing money is a process that requires specialized knowledge and prudent research. This is achievable only if a well-organized documentation system is in place. Systematic record keeping not just improves your efficacy, but also have a lasting positive impact on your financial behaviors. So, you should get into the habit of keeping organized records as early as possible in your life. Getting organized is not just a state to arrive at, but also a way of managing your financial affairs. Getting organized is both a process and an attitude. It should become a second nature.

Probably the draggiest, but arguably the central, feature of money management is day-to-day record keeping. It can help you save time and money while giving you peace of mind. I hope that above-mentioned techniques in tandem with your wisdom can play a big role in making your record keeping system as undemanding as possible.

2.3 Evaluating Your Financial Health

To succeed in your wealth creation endeavor, first you have to get the true picture of your current financial standing. Evaluating your financial health is apparently the least exciting part of the money management process. But then, it is the initial and essential element of the process as it details your present financial position that forms the basis for other elements of the wealth creation process. So, it is important to analytically evaluate your current financial status before progressing to other aspects of money management. Moreover, your present panoptic picture will help you in planning and securing a stronger financial future.

Personal Financial Status (PFS)

Your personal financial status report compares what you own with what you owe. It is simply an abstract of your financial standing, i.e., your assets and your liabilities. It is often referred to as balance sheet, personal balance sheet, personal financial statement or net worth statement. I may be at ease with these titles because of my professional credentials in the field but these may not encourage an uninitiated person due to the anecdotal qualms associated with these titles owing to use or abuse of accounting terminology of business organizations. Secondly, these titles are likely to baffle a nonprofessional as accounting practices and analytical tools in the corporate world are quite advanced whereas this is not the case in the personal domain, wherein effective money management techniques are just emerging. Therefore, we prefer to use the term personal financial status, which is a simple, descriptive and comforting title.

Personal financial status (PFS) simply depicts three modules — assets, liabilities, and net assets or net worth which is essentially the difference between assets and liabilities. Here our objective is not to just prepare a simple list of assets and liabilities, but to device an effective mechanism that analytically monitors our financial health as well as prompt us to take our monetary decisions responsibly. To facilitate this we are applying the coding structure discussed in the previous chapter in the following sample illustration wherein assets are valued at the prevailing market prices and liabilities at the net payable amount to get a realistic view of the financial status.

Personal Financial Status Worksheet
of Ms. S.Ample as on 01.01.12

Code	Description	Amount ($)	Amount ($)
1	ASSETS		
1.1	Liquid Financial Assets:-		311000
1.11	Cash	4500	
1.12	Bank Balances	55000	
1.13	Fixed Return Instruments	250000	
…..	…..		
1.19	Miscellaneous	1500	
1.2	Other Financial Investments:-		1650000
1.21	Equity	450000	
1.22	Bonds	150000	
1.23	Commodities	-	
1.24	Mutual Funds	875000	
1.25	Insurance- Present Value	150000	
…..	……		
1.29	Miscellaneous	25000	
1.3	Physical Assets:-		2520000
1.31	Home	2500000	
1.32	Real Estate Investments	-	

cont. >>

Code	Description	Amount ($)	Amount ($)
1.33	Precious Metals	-	
1.34	Artworks	15000	
…..	…..		
1.39	Miscellaneous	5000	
1.4	Personal Assets:-		1006000
1.41	Vehicles	350000	
1.42	Gadgets/ Appliances	250000	
1.43	Jewelry/ Precious Metals	300000	
1.44	Artwork	18500	
…..	…..		
1.49	Miscellaneous	87500	
1.9	Other Assets:-		370000
1.91	Business	360000	
…..	…..		
1.99	Miscellaneous	10000	
1	**TOTAL ASSETS**		**5857000**
1.0	Deferred Assets		
1.01	Retirement Plans worth	150000	
1.02	Royalty on Books	7500	
…..	…….		
1.09	Miscellaneous	3500	
2	**LIABILITIES**		
2.1	Current Liabilities:-		52000

Code	Description	Amount ($)	Amount ($)
2.11	Budgeted Household Expenses	17500	
2.12	Other Budgeted Expenses	7500	
2.13	Installments Payable	10500	
2.14	Mortgage repayments	15000	
.....			
2.19	Miscellaneous	1500	
	Long-Term Liabilities:-		
2.2	Against Financial Investments:-		130000
2.21	Equity	55000	
2.22	Bonds	-	
2.23	Commodities	-	
2.24	Mutual Funds	75000	
2.25	Present value of Insurance	-	
.....	......		
2.29	Miscellaneous	-	
2.3	Against Physical Assets:-		1500000
2.31	Home	1500000	
2.32	Real Estate Investments	-	
2.33	Precious Metals	-	
2.34	Artworks	-	
.....	.....		
2.39	Miscellaneous	-	
2.4	Against Personal Assets:-		200000

Code	Description	Amount ($)	Amount ($)
2.41	Vehicles	200000	
2.42	Gadgets/ Appliances	-	
2.43	Jewelry/ Precious Metals	-	
2.44	Artwork	-	
…..	…..		
2.49	Miscellaneous	-	
2.5	Other Liabilities		750000
2.51	Personal Loan	450000	
2.52	Education Loan	250000	
…..	…..		
2.59	Miscellaneous	50000	
2.9	Liabilities against Other Assets:-	-	
2	**TOTAL Liabilities**		2632000
2.0	Contingent Liabilities:-		-
1-2	**NET ASSETS** (Assets-Liabilities)		3225000

Even though the sample PFS depicted in the above table is self-explanatory and the procedure is clear-cut and flexible enough to meet the requirements of nearly everyone, we prefer to shed some light on some components of the personal financial status using the following pointers.

+   1.1:- Liquid financial assets consists of cash and cash equivalent assets, which are not primarily for return purposes. Amount earmarked for the emergency fund can be appropriated to the miscellaneous subcategory. Alternatively, it can be deployed in the cash equivalent fixed return products.

+   1.2:- Other financial investments are essentially the financial assets but may include investments in tangible assets such as commodities, real estate and gold via the mutual funds route. You may like to insert additional columns for recording purchase price and other relevant details to facilitate future analysis.

+   1.3:- Physical assets encompass all non-financial tangible assets that are primarily acquired for investment purposes. Due to this reason, some people prefer to exclude their home from this category and take it in the personal assets category. A few even opt to exclude it altogether from the personal financial status. If you include it, subtract at least five percent from the market price for commission and other sales expenses.

+   1.4:- Personal assets cover all possessions intended for personal or family use including vehicles, yacht, computers, equipments, etc., which are not necessarily assets in the true sense as they decrease in value with time and generally do not bring in any income. Tangible assets such as artworks and precious metals purchased mainly for profit should be included under the physical assets category. However, such assets can be classified in the personal assets category if they are primarily acquired for their esteem value.

+   1.9:- Assets having present worth and not covered in any other category can be stated here. Be realistic particularly in valuing these assets. Some people mistakenly consider probable future inheritance in this category, which is not correct. If you still insist, future inheritance can be exhibited under deferred assets (i.e., 1.0) because your personal financial status is meant to examine only assets and loans you have right now.

+   1.0:- Deferred assets should not be considered a part of the PFS, as they do not have current value. However, they should be expressed notionally under this category so that their importance in the future planning is adequately appreciated.

−   2.1:- Current liabilities include all payouts for the month including installments payable for the near month on the personal loans and mortgages. However, the balance debt on these should be reflected against the related assets. Some people favor to take in installments for the next three/six months in this category. This seems unwarranted especially when a reasonable amount is set aside in the emergency fund. Keep in mind that this category is designed primarily for personal and household expenses and as such, any repayments on account of loans taken for investment purposes should not be reflected here.

- 2.2:- All outstanding loans taken to finance the financial assets pertaining to the category 1.2 ought to be shown here. Special attention is to be given to the leveraged positions in the derivatives segments of equity, commodities and the like since these instruments are intrinsically highly leveraged. So you should consider gross value of the investments under assets (1.2) and the same value after adjusting for the margins paid under this category. It may be incongruous here, but I would strongly urge the employed people especially the uninitiated ones to shun these speculative instruments completely.

- 2.3:- This category consists of loans taken for acquiring physical assets including mortgage for real estate assets. In most of the cases, house is the biggest asset and the mortgage for the same is the biggest liability. Some people prefer to show only capital amount outstanding in the financial status and some favor to take in the entire sum payable including the interest component. Line of reasoning offered by the conservatives in favor of the second option is that amount payable is virtually defined whereas underlying asset can appreciate or depreciate. Therefore, the treatment of mortgage or outstanding loan is to be carefully deliberated, as there could be substantial impact on your net worth calculations.

- 2.4:- Loans taken for purchase of personal worldly goods such as cars and computers are shown here. You should appreciate that many of these assets depreciate with time while the outstanding loans may increase. In contrast, artwork, gold, jewelry, etc. can be regarded as good investments if appreciation returns exceed rate of interest.

- 2.5:- Other liabilities reflect advances not covered in any of the above categories and mainly consist of loans taken to fulfill personal or family needs and wants. These debts do not create any asset yet some of these such as education loan, marriage loan and the like can turn out to be the best investments yielding lifelong dividends. On the contrary, some of these loans may result in squandering of capital for extravagant spending. Caution is warranted in availing such loans because unnecessary exploitation of these facilities can lead to spendthrift tendencies, which often get in the way of the better money management practices.

- 2.0:- Contingent liabilities include probable future payouts, which cannot be ascertained or quantified. Some people erroneously show alimony, as per premarital agreement or otherwise in this category often triggering prejudicial way of thinking.

✓ 1-2:- Net assets indicate the difference between assets and liabilities. This reflects the factual capital that truly belongs to you, thus giving you a better understanding of your present financial health. It is commonly referred as net worth. We prefer to use the term net assets as it connotes the literal sense of ownership as well as facilitates an analytical way of perceiving things. Further, it puts the assets valuation in the right perspective, particularly the financed assets. Net Assets figure provides a reference point on your financial road map, which you can use along with your financial vision to formulate appropriate strategies to reach your destination. It is usually positive, but when it is negative, i.e., you are in debt, the important thing is to make earnest improvements in your financial conduct to turn it around at the earliest. First, you have to make a plan to break the shackles of the debt trap so that you can resume your march to a secured financial future.

Analysis of Personal Financial Status

While some people shy away from number crunching, others tend to spend a lot of time in ad hoc thinking to analyze their finances, perhaps in a vague manner. Even these off the cuff exercises have an important and positive effect on their money management endeavors, which cannot be fully attributed to the placebo effect. Nevertheless, it is always better to adapt a structured approach rather than aimlessly dabbling in our financial affairs.

However, in the personal finance domain, there is a real dearth of effective analytical tools and techniques to put into action the dependable money management practices. Besides, the analytical techniques ought to be simple enough to serve the needs of laypersons. Furthermore, to make the matters a bit tricky, usual parameters in the personal money management practices are clearly deficient in the standardization aspect. So, if you consult n number of personal financial planners, you are likely to get n number of recommendations, many of which may possibly be inconsistent or even contradictory to each other.

Notwithstanding these limitations, it is imperative for all of us to check our financial health regularly, as we do in the case of our health checkups. There are hundreds of diagnostic health checkups available, but usually a person may not require even half a dozen for her/his medical examination. Like wise, we scarcely use more than a dozen pertinent indicators in any specific case from a repertoire of more than a hundred indicators for analyzing financial health of a person. Talking about all these carries the risk of overwhelming the readers and as such can be counterproductive to the intended intent of this book. So we are imparting here some important pointers, which have the potential to serve the purpose of nearly all the people aspiring to manage their money proactively and wisely.

Quantifying Components of PFS

Your net assets figure give a handy indicator of your financial health, but does not offer any guidance to analyze the causes and consequences that can provide a direction to realign and modify your financial strategies so as to ultimately measure up to your vision. Therefore, net assets figure requires further examination to confirm that various components are in harmony with the short term and long term goals, and the wealth is rightly distributed among various asset classes. Moreover, this exercise supplements your long-term vision and provides short-term motivation.

So here, we require a basic mechanism to decipher the components of our net assets so that we can manage our financial affairs in a much better way and take positive steps towards improving it. It is worthwhile to quantify all the main categories of our wealth to make a discerning assessment of our owned assets. This we can easily do by subtracting liability categories from the corresponding asset categories as depicted in the PFS table wherein our assets and connected liabilities are properly aligned and represented by analogous codes. This seemingly simple coding structure is versatile enough to facilitate many such functional features as well as other logical thinking aspects. We are exemplifying hereunder the computation of components of PFS in absolute as well as percentage terms. Let us incorporate the above-mentioned figures of PFS into a hypothetical illustration to tabulate the percentage analysis of various components of the net assets.

Percentage Analysis of Net Assets

Formula		Description	Amount ($)	% Net Assets
1.1	minus	Net Liquid Financial	259000	8
2.1		Assets		
1.2	minus	Net Financial	1520000	47
2.2		Investments		
1.3	minus	Net Physical Assets	1020000	32
2.3				
1.4	minus	Net Personal Assets	806000	25
2.4				
1.5	minus	Net Other Liabilities	-380000	-12
2.5				
1 minus 2		**NET ASSETS**	3225000	100

We can take this analysis a step further to examine minutely the constituents of all major categories, as depicted in the following illustration.

Asset Wise Analysis of Wealth

Calculation	Description	Amount ($)	% of Net Assets
1.2? - 2.2?	**Net Financial Investments :**	**1520000**	**47**
1.21 - 2.21	Net Equity	395000	12.25
1.22 - 2.22	Net Bonds	150000	4.65
1.23 - 2.23	Net Commodities	-	-
1.24 - 2.24	Net Mutual Funds	800000	24.81
1.25 - 2.25	Insurance-Net Value	150000	4.65
..... -	......		
1.29 - 2.29	Net Miscellaneous	25000	0.78
1.3? - 2.3?	**Net Physical Assets**	**1020000**	**32**
1.31 - 2.31	Home	1000000	31.01
1.32 - 2.32	Real Estate Investments	-	-
1.33 - 2.33	Precious Metals	-	-
1.34 - 2.34	Artworks	15000	0.47
..... -	......		
1.39 - 2.39	Miscellaneous	5000	0.16
1.4? - 2.4?	**Net Personal Assets**	**806000**	**25**
1.41 - 2.41	Vehicles	150000	4.65
1.42 - 2.42	Gadgets/ Appliances	250000	7.75
1.43 - 2.43	Jewelry/Precious Metals	300000	9.30
1.44 - 2.44	Artwork	18500	0.57
..... -	......		
1.49 - 2.49	Miscellaneous	87500	2.11

Further, we may choose to scan our major assets at micro level to interpret more intelligibly our factual investment status to derive the insights needed for wealth creation. We elucidate this with a hypothetical example.

Analysis of Equity Holdings

Equity Components	Amount ($)	% of Equity
Equity-Value Stocks:		
Large Cap		
Mid Cap		
Small Cap		
Equity-Growth Stocks:		
Large Cap		
Mid Cap		
Small Cap		
Equity Indices:		
Derivatives:		
Total Equity	395000	100

We will address analysis of equity holdings in detail while discussing investment planning. The above is just to get a break up of the equity holdings. Likewise, we can carry out this exercise for other major assets to check out our financial wherewithal more clearly.

While quantifying PFS, we have reckoned the net assets figure a positive one. At times, it can be a negative figure. A negative net assets figure is a serious issue, which demands immediate correction course to rectify the accumulated anomalies of the past. It also calls for a plan to ensure that similar situation do not occur in future.

Measuring Liquidity

To propitiate financial concerns in day-to-day life, we need to know our ability to meet necessary expenses and maturing obligations as they become due. It is important to know our solvency levels because it is not just mentally relieving, but it also provides us an option to deploy surplus funds in a more profitable manner. The most important solvency ratio is to ensure a reasonable cover for monthly expenses. There are many liquidity ratios, which can be suitably personalized to focus on our specific financial issues. Some are outlined hereunder with reference to the above PFS example wherein current liabilities (2.1) correspond to the monthly payouts.

1. Monthly Expenses Cover:
Liquid assets (1.1) ÷ Current Liabilities (2.1) =

$311000 \div 52000 = 5.98 \approx 6$ times

While planning career transition or any other major lifetime event, it is worthwhile to compute this ratio by taking all financial assets (1.1+1.2) as follows.
[Liquid assets (1.1) + Other Financial Assets (1.2)] ÷ Current

Liabilities (2.1) = $[311000+1650000] \div 52000 = 37.71 \approx 38$ times

Some people prefer to adapt a conservative approach and as such calculate this factor of safety after adjusting other liabilities (2.5) or net other liabilities (1.5-2.5) from the above equation.
[Liquid assets (1.1) + Other Financial Assets (1.2) - Other Liabilities

(2.5)] ÷ Current Liabilities (2.1) =

$[311000+1650000-750000] \div 52000 = 23.29 \approx 23$ times

[Liquid assets (1.1) + Other Financial Assets (1.2) - Net Other

Liabilities (1.5-2.5)] ÷ Current Liabilities (2.1) =

$[311000+1650000-380000] \div 52000 = 30.40 \approx 30$ times

2. Debt Burden:
The following ratios can be applied to calculate the debt status at aggregate level.
A) Total liabilities to total assets:

Total Liabilities (2) ÷ Total Assets (1) = $2632000 \div 5857000 = 0.45 = 45\%$

B) Net assets to total assets:

Net Assets (1-2) ÷ Total Assets (1) = $(5857000-2632000) \div 5857000 =$

$3225000 \div 5857000 = 0.55 = 55\%$

C) Personal debt cover: Debt burden relating to other liabilities mainly personal and education loans need to be viewed with reference to liquid plus other financial assets.

Personal Loans (2.5) ÷ [Liquid Financial Assets (1.1) + Other Financial Assets (2.2)] =

750000÷ [311000+1650000] = 38%

To ensure that personal debt is within reasonable limit and not a serious drag on the wealth creation endeavors, it should also be compared with reference to the monthly income as well as monthly savings.

D) Debt vs. Asset analysis: To conduct debt analysis at each major asset level, we can follow the following example that clearly depicts the debt percentages for all major assets.

Debt Analysis at Assets Level

Assets	Asset Value- $	Loan Amount- $	Formula (Calculation)	Debt %
Equity	450000	55000	2.21÷1.21	12
Mutual Funds	875000	75000	2.24÷1.24	9
Home	2500000	1500000	2.31÷1.31	60
Vehicles	350000	200000	2.41÷1.41	57
TOTAL	5857000	2632000	2÷1	45

Inflation Defense

It is important to appreciate that not all the assets provide an adequate cover against inflation. When we have significant portion of our net assets in personal assets, such as vehicles, gadgets and computers, which depreciate with time and do not provide protection against inflation, our financial status cannot be reckoned as good enough. We need to assess the share of appreciating assets in our net assets to determine our protection level against inflation. Appreciating assets are those investments where we expect capital appreciation in line with or more than inflation. A simple ratio to calculate inflation protection level is as follows.

[Other Financial Assets (1.2)+Physical Assets(2.2)] ÷Net Assets(1-2)

[1650000 + 2520000] ÷ 3225000 = 1.29 times

Being a conjectural parameter and for the sake of simplicity, we have overlooked some assets such as fixed income instruments (1.13), business investments (1.91) and appreciating personal assets (1.43 &1.44) from this calculation. Some people consider fixed income securities as a hedge against inflation since these securities are likely to provide returns in line with inflation if not better. However, some people tend to ignore all fixed return instruments as well as personal assets except for precious metals and artworks to arrive at a more comforting assessment of the inflation shield.

Then again, some people prefer to ignore their home as well as mortgage from this calculation. They appreciate the fact that the value of home may increase or decrease but mortgage will definitely include the interest component. Because home is generally the biggest asset, excluding it from the calculation will significantly lower the inflation ratio, which may perhaps be misleading.

Periodic Progress

Above-mentioned indicators are more of a revealing nature essentially geared to soothe our nerves besides preparing us well for the probable contingencies. We need to further check the progress in our financial status at regular intervals to monitor our progress towards our envisioned goals. This can be done just by adding columns for periods under consideration in the PFS. Simply scanning our financial status for several years would give us the direction and the insight for the prospective course of action. We should carry out this exercise at least once a year to get an idea of our progress and to identify the areas where we may need to fine-tune our investment strategies. In addition to making year wise PFS, we should examine the variations in net assets components minutely between the two periods. This is clarified in the following tables.

Periodic Progress Worksheet
(Year wise Variation in Financial Status)

Formula	Assets Category	Amount as on 01.01.12 ($)	Amount as on 01.01.13 ($)	Vari-ation %
1.2? - 2.2?	Net Financial Investments :	1520000	1738000	14
1.21 - 2.21	Net Equity	395000	543000	45
1.22 - 2.22	Net Bonds	150000	150000	-
1.23 - 2.23	Net Commodities	-	-	
1.24 - 2.24	Net Mutual Funds	800000	850000	6
1.25 - 2.25	Net Value of Insurance	150000	170000	13
..... -	......			
1.29 - 2.29	Net Miscellaneous	25000	25000	-
1.3? - 2.3?	Net Physical Assets	1020000	1410000	38
1.31 - 2.31	Net Home	1000000	1390000	39
1.32 - 2.32	Net Real Estate Investments	-	-	
1.33 - 2.33	Net Precious Metals	-	-	
1.34 - 2.34	Net Artworks	15000	20000	33
..... -	.....			
1.39 - 2.39	Net Miscellaneous	5000		-
1.4? - 2.4?	Net Personal Assets	806000	636000	-21
1.41 - 2.41	Net Vehicles	150000	100000	-33
1.42 - 2.42	...			
1.43 - 2.43	Net Jewelry/ Precious Metals	550000	450000	-18
1.44 - 2.44	Net Artwork	18500	18500	-
..... -	.....			
1.49 - 2.49	Net Miscellaneous	87500	67500	-23

Furthermore, we should break down the aberrant and major variations to pinpoint the reasons along these lines. This will give us a clear-cut perception of the variance as well as prompt us to initiate the right course of action so as to maximize our future returns.

Asset Wise Analysis of Major Variations

Particulars	Net Equity- $ (1.21 - 2.21)	Home- $ (1.31 - 2.31)
As on 01.01.12:		
A. Market Value	450000	2500000
B. Less loans	-55000	1500000
C. Net Value- 2012	**395000**	**1000000**
During the year:		
D. Additions+	40000	0
E. Loan repaid+	55000	90000
F. Loan taken-	0	0
G. Sold-	-55000	0
H. Net at the year end	435000	1090000
As on 01.01.13:		
I. Market Value	543000	2800000
J. Less loans	0	1410000
K. Net Value- 2013	**543000**	**1390000**
L. Appreciation(K-H)	108000	300000
M.Interest paid	2000	90000
N. Net Appreciation(L-M)	**106000**	**210000**
O. Appreciation-%	24%	8%
P. Previous Year +/-	5%	12%
Next Year Expectation	?	?
Next Year Strategy	…..	…..
	…..	…..

You might be wondering about the acceptable benchmarks in respect of the above-mentioned indicators, as is the case with the health check ups. Our intent to refrain from sounding overly prescriptive is not the only reason to skip the discussion on the standard yardsticks to judge the financial health. In fact, when it comes to establishing universal benchmarks, financial health monitoring is a bit perplexing and is widely divergent to physical health diagnostics. Incidentally, it may fall behind physical health in this respect but otherwise assures better financial health in times to come unlike physical health, which has to deteriorate with time. Secondly, we desist from specifying universal standards because each case is unique and interplay of multiple variables calls for a subjective analysis to decide what is truly right and not just apparently right. Even specifying guidelines to set standards is not favored since you and/or your advisor can only determine your comfort level as well as your realistic financial vision. In all probability when you diligently undertake your money management, you can decide what is best for you taking into account all the relevant personal data.

Scrutiny of PFS is not a one-off exercise. It demands periodic analysis, especially in conjunction with your promising goals to monitor whether your strategies are working in harmony with your vision. At this stage, you are not supposed to devote too much time on the analysis part. As we take up other elements of the financial vision process, you will come across many worthwhile indicators to assist you in the art and science of wealth creation.

People, who do not have conviction in their Vision, occasionally get worked up in the implementation process. This is primarily because they fail to put the efforts required to realize their vision in the right perspective, as they just close the eyes to compare the efforts they put to earn money. You should not take the money management as drudgery. Think about the effort-reward ratio to perk you up. This is a moneymaking game that you have to play earnestly to win. Anyway, if you still feel overwhelmed, you may take the help of your personal financial advisor or write to us*.

---

* If you would like a personalized template to help you make your own Personal Financial Status, please contact us.

2.4 Improving Your Financial Health: Spending Wisely, Saving Smartly

By now, you know where you are and where you want to go. Now you have to decide how to undertake this journey to your dream destination, i.e., your financial vision. To reach your coveted destination quickly and easily, you need to devise a simple mechanism to manage your finances on a day-to-day basis.

Today's cutthroat existence leaves us with no time to look at our routine money matters in a detailed manner. This chapter seeks to address this issue as well as explore our financial fitness regimen by examining how we earn, spend and save. This chapter will also illustrate efficient tools and effective techniques that facilitate productive monitoring of our money matters.

Most of us adopt a careful and cost-conscious approach to our routine money matters. We endure our mundane money maneuvers with presumed deftness, as we take our financial decisions of our own free will. Occasionally, we may succumb to the temptations of impulse buying, ostensibly under societal pressures and others' influence. Such behavior probably is more a sin of omission than commission, but it often occurs. Yet, we cannot take refuge in real or imaginary pressures for these abnormal spendthrift actions, as only we are accountable to ourselves as well as to our loved ones for a secured financial future. However, the best way to get rid of temptations to impulse purchases is to indulge in envisioning financial goals on a regular basis.

We humans usually take spending decisions on conviction, which may or may not be based on sound reasons. Invariably our financial decisions, small or large, have roots in our instinctive faith in the right or apparently right reasons. But there could be a big difference between a right decision and an apparently right decision, which may clear up much later only at the post mortem stage. So, it is advisable to adapt an adaptable and true to life mechanism to take out the whimsicality from our important monetary decisions. This mechanism may not always bring in huge wealth, but it can surely avert probable financial hardships and help you to stay on the course even during hard times. Before we proceed to put in place a comprehensive yet simple mechanism to regulate our routine financial matters, here we sum up the main benefits of such a financial fitness mechanism.

✓ It provides a workable spending and savings plan to give you control of your money management.
✓ It inculcates the discipline of forced savings and restricts the impulse buying.
✓ It gives a realistic and flexible plan to meet expenses.
✓ It abates money matters anxiety and gives you financial peace of mind.
✓ It provides the necessary purpose, direction and a yardstick to monitor your financial progress.
✓ It facilitates you to build assets as well as improve your standard of living.
✓ It helps you to adapt a balanced approach in day-to-day money matters.
✓ It gives you an opportunity to align your money management with your financial vision.
✓ It makes you the master so that you manage the money rather than money managing you.
✓ It helps you to stop worrying about money and start enjoying your money.

The financial fitness mechanism deals with three statements, namely, income account, personal budget and cash flow. The ingredients of all these statements are more or less the same. Our routine money management mechanism is different from the usual method of clubbing all receipts as incomes and all payments as expenses in the income account, personal budget and cash flow. Many personal financial advisors tend to consider all receipts, such as salary, profit, interest, dividend and suchlike takings as income in the income account. Some even take sale proceeds of investments and such other capital receipts into the income category. Likewise, all payouts such as household expenses, mortgage, loan repayments of all sorts, interest, et cetera are clubbed as expenses. This approach leads to a seemingly simple tabular array of all money transactions in one assorted account. This deceptively down-to-earth method, however, may not serve the intended purpose of getting the best from the finite resources to create wealth because it restricts the analytical thinking or makes it somewhat cumbersome. A systematic and truly functional mechanism may require a few minutes extra initially to clearly differentiate all receipts and payments between capital and revenue, but will definitely simplify the analysis part as well as encourage the right financial conduct forever, particularly when it comes to allocating finances to avertable spending or desirable savings. Rather than taking up a disquisition on the pros and cons of the methodologies, we straightaway take up how to distinguish between capital and revenue in our money matters. Before we discuss the income account, it is essential to understand the concept of revenue and capital in the context of personal money management in order to adapt sound financial practices. As a rule of thumb, receipts and payments can be generally classified as capital or revenue as per the following broad pointers.

✓ Generally, capital refers to long-term and revenue relates to the period.
✓ Capital is destined for future needs whereas revenue is meant for current needs.
✓ Capital receipts are tax exempt but revenue receipts are charged to tax.
✓ Capital expenses are one time while revenue expenses are recurring.
✓ Capital signifies a fund whereas revenue refers to a flow.

In the financial vision context, revenue broadly relates to maintaining the desirable standard of living from the current income while capital transactions are usually meant for future needs and wealth creation goals. Though returns on investments may be considered as revenue income for tax purposes, we prefer to treat such earnings as capital income since these yields are predominantly on account of capital investments and not as a consequence of our exertions. But then, both are equally important to realize our financial vision, as they are interlinked and interdependent on each other. When managed astutely, they not only feed each other but also build on each other.

Now we return to our financial fitness mechanism to discuss the income statement, which is the key to everlasting financial well-being. We are deliberately keeping the mechanism simple, as a complex mechanism is likely to stultify the implementation as well as lower the utility quotient. Secondly, a complex process cannot be either endearing or enduring in the long haul. Further to make the process a wieldy one, we may decide to ignore all transactions up to a fixed amount say $ 10 or 0.1 % of our income and create an inconsequential category that can be a balancing figure to simplify the process. You may fix any amount that is not significant for you as long as total of inconsequential category is within acceptable limits, say 2% of your income. It has to be your decision considering your financial condition and monetary attitude. With a view to make it easy to espouse the modular approach in all the areas of our financial fitness regimen, here we discuss the components of the income account.

Income Account

The personal income account quantifies the financial transactions over a specific period. It is a snapshot of a person's financial activities comprising income earned and mundane expenditure incurred. It is generally prepared on a monthly basis to monitor the financial discipline in day-to-day life. It helps us to estimate the surplus/deficit, i.e., the difference between the income and the expenses. The income account covers three main parts: income, expenses and net earnings. The income part needs to be segregated into earned income and capital income to facilitate clear demarcation between revenue and capital.

Earned Income

This revenue income module covers all remuneration arising from our occupation wherein the income accrues primarily because of our hard work. Be it employment, self-employment, or a mix of both. These earnings invariably pertain to a specific period, thus making it convenient to organize money management for that period. These receipts have nothing to do with our investments or assets. So it is more prudent to treat these earnings as an entirely separate unit distinct from returns on assets. These are meant for regular household expenses and savings. For that reason this category is assigned the distinct code prefix I as depicted in the following table.

Earned Income Table for the Month

Code	Description	Amount ($)
I	Earned Income:	
I.1	Salary	45000
I.2	Incentives	10000
I.3	Bonus	5000
... ...		
I.7	Business Income	
I.8	Royalty on books	750
I.9	Miscellaneous	250
I	TOTAL	61000

Capital Income

This module includes various receipts, which accrue essentially on account of owned assets. These are usually returns on investments and net proceeds from the sale of assets. Return proceeds are attributable to personal financial status and as such, this separate module for capital receipts facilitates clear demarcation of funds intended for long-term plans. The following table shows separately the return receipts and capital proceeds.

Capital Income Table for the Month

Code	Description	Return Amount ($)	Capital Amount ($)
3	**Capital/Returns Income**		
3.12	Bank Balances	100	
3.13	Fixed Return Instruments	1000	
3.21	Equity	1500	7500
3.22	Bonds	1000	
3.24	Mutual Funds	4000	
3.33	Precious Metals		150000
3.34	Artworks		
3.91	Business	4000	
.....	.....		
3.99	Miscellaneous	100	
3	**TOTAL**	**11700**	**157500**

Expenses

The next part of income account deals with expenses. Monthly monitoring of expenses may not apparently yield sizeable rewards, yet ultimate financial outcomes largely depend on how we manage our day-to-day expenses. We are not advocating arbitrary curtailing of expenses, as it can be counterproductive. Studies on consumer behaviors indicate that people, who exercise excessive self-control on expending, are prone to make more impulse-purchases as and when they get the opportunities. All we are suggesting is that we need to take our expenses a bit seriously, and while doing so, we must remember that the biggest room is the room for saving. We can afford to downplay the loose change but not the greenbacks. However, we may not record an expense, which is less than the inconsequential limit fixed by us. The idea is to save our valuable time, which is definitely a finite and valuable resource. Even at the cost of sounding inconsistent, the dynamic process of financial vision requires us to suggest that we should not consider even small expenses as chicken feed because there is no easy money in life.

A formal mechanism to account for expenses not just infuses financial discipline, but also inculcates right spending habits. With a view to keep an eye on expenses, experts prefer to classify them as fixed or variable, controllable or uncontrollable, desirable or undesirable and so on. Our versatile modular approach makes it easy to adapt any preferred method of classification. Let us now explore the various expense categories in the following sample modules:

EXPLORING CATEGORY-WISE EXPENSES

E.L = Living Expenses:

Code	Expenses Group	Monthly Amount ($)	Annual Amount ($) (optional)
E.L1	Essential groceries		
E.L2	Other groceries		
E.L3	Other essential supplies		
E.L4	Other discretionary supplies		
E.L5	Essential clothing		
E.L6	Education expenses		
E.L...	... ...		
E.L8	Pet care supplies		
E.L99	Miscellaneous living		
E.L.	**TOTAL**		

E.D = Personal Debt Expenses:

Code	Expenses Group	Monthly Amount	Annual Amount (optional)
E.D1	Credit Cards- EMI		
E.D2	Personal Loans		
E.D3	Education Loan		
E.D4	Charity Contributions		
E.D5	... ...		
E.D			
E.D			
E.D99	Other Obligations		
E.D.	**TOTAL**		

E.H = Housing Expenses:

Code	Expenses Group	Monthly Amount	Annual Amount (optional)
E.H1	Rent		
E.H2	Mortgage		
E.H3	Insurance/Taxes		
E.H4	Electricity/ Water		
E.H5	Phone/ Cable/Internet		
E.H6	House Cleaning Services		
E.H..	... ...		
E.H8	Maintenance		
E.H99	Other housing expenses		
E.H.	**TOTAL**		

E.F = Family Care Expenses:

Code	Expenses Group	Monthly Amount	Annual Amount (optional)
E.F1	Life insurance		
E.F2	Health/ Medical Insurance		
E.F3	Doctors' fees		
E.F4	Prescription Medicines		
E.F5	Other Supplements		
E.F6	Dentist/ Eye Care		
E.F7	Health Club		
E.F99	Misc. Family Care Expenses		
E.F.	**TOTAL**		

E.T = Transport Expenses:

Code	Expenses Group	Monthly Amount	Annual Amount (optional)
E.T1	Vehicle Loans		
E.T2	Taxes/Insurance		
E.T3	Gasoline/Oil etc.		
E.T4	Repair & Maintenance		
E.T5	Parking/ Toll fees		
E.T.	… …		
E.T99	Other Transport Expenses		
E.T.	**TOTAL**		

E.R = Recreational Expenses:

Code	Expenses Group	Monthly Amount	Annual Amount (optional)
E.R1	Movies/ Dining out		
E.R2	Anniversaries/ Birthdays		
E.R3	Weekends/Holidays Outings		
E.R4	Discretionary Clothing		
E.R5	Gifts/ Impulse Buying		
E.R6	Vacation Trip	1000	12000
E.R...	... .		
E.R99	Other Recreational Expenses		
E.R.	**TOTAL**		

E.M = Miscellaneous Expenses:

Code	Expenses Group	Monthly Amount	Annual Amount (optional)
E.M	Inconsequential category		
E.M	Gadgets/Computers etc.		
E.M	PC/Appliances Supplies		
E.M	Repair & Maintenance		
E.M	Other Misc. Expenses		
E.M.	**TOTAL**		

After appreciating the modular approach in respect of the above-mentioned expenses and incomes, let us revert to the income account. A usable format of the income account is illustrated in the following table, which depicts just the outlines of the above modules to facilitate a clear-cut construal of the big picture. The last column of the table shows indicative benchmark ranges for the various expense heads. These benchmarks ought to be as dynamic as an individual's circumstances. So, these should not be considered as inviolable because only you and your unique context can endorse the model yardsticks. The adage 'with experience comes knowledge' is very much applicable here. Moreover, even your model benchmarks change over a period since your income and expense fluctuate as you brave out various phases of the life cycle.

Monthly Income and Expense Analysis

Code	Monthly Total	Amount	Income %	Target Range in %
I	Revenue Income		100	
E.L.	Living Expenses			25-35
E.D.	Personal debt Expenses			10-20
E.H.	Housing Expenses			25-35
E.F.	Family Care Expenses			5-15
E.T.	Transport Expenses			5-15
E.R.	Recreational Expenses			3-10
E.M.	Misc. Expenses			2-5
E.	Total Expenses			
I-E	Net Earnings Surplus/Deficit			5-25
3	Returns Income			
3 + (I-E)	Long term Funds			

You can make your financial fitness program more effective as well as interesting by suitably fine-tuning the various modules. Here are some pointers on what you need to keep in mind while personalizing the abovementioned modules to serve your specific requirements.

1. You have to simplify your income account as much as you deem fit in order to make it a flexible, adaptive, dynamic and time efficient process. You may follow ABC analysis along with classifying the incomes and expenses in the controllable and uncontrollable groups to make things easier. However, you may opt for as elaborate account as you want in any one or more of the modules as per your needs.

2. While earned income for the period are expendable, capital incomes including returns on investments are ideally aimed at wealth creation.

3. Depending on your circumstances, you should earmark a reasonable portion of earned income for future goals.

4. The profits from business should be segregated into two parts— return on capital employed and the remainder. Return on the capital should be taken in the capital income module and the balance in the Earned Income module.

5. Depending on your financial goals, you may decide to focus on augmenting the income side or keeping in check the expenses during a particular period. Preferably, you should strike the right balance between the two.

6. Only house mortgage, vehicle and other personal loans repayments should be considered as expenses for the period. However, if your mortgage repayment amount is high, you may consider only rent equivalent amount as monthly expenses and the remainder as investment in real estate.

7. Miscellaneous expenses category is for the residual expenses, which do not warrant much attention. The main reason for the miscellaneous expenses is simplification, however care should be taken to ensure that major expenses are not classified here because it shows poor working and hinders analysis.

8. Annual sizeable expenses such as holiday trip should be divided in twelve months. Similarly, convert other occasional expenses to the monthly format.
9. While establishing benchmarks for monitoring spending and savings, doing your own research is the right way. With time, this will give you good sense to set the realistic yardsticks.
10. Be sure to ensure that net earnings are within desirable range. If consistently net earnings are not as anticipated, then you need to review your income account thoroughly to realign it with your financial objectives.

There are several ways to make as well as monitor the income account. You can do it yourself in a spreadsheet or a good old notebook. Companies of all sizes and specialty are offering money management products. These products are either too basic to accommodate your specific issues or too elaborate whereby making them unworkable in the long haul. Secondly, these products are often developed with a very wide horizon in mind, as a result, ease of use and configurability potential suffer. You can easily establish your own tailor-made program, which will not just address all your concerns but also provide you a flexible, interesting and timesaving process. However, if you feel somewhat overwhelmed, you may start with just the final table of monthly income and expense analysis in conjunction with the time tested basic envelopes method that entails keeping money in separate envelops for the various expense categories and recording all payouts on the envelops or stuffing receipts in the envelopes for reconciliation at a later stage. Even this basic system will help you to turn strategic insights into tactical action aimed at realizing your financial goals.

Personal Budget

The income account carries the risk of being dumped midway because it is often viewed as a sort of post-mortem exercise. In the absence of a measuring yardstick, such an apprehension seems justified. So, we take up the personal budget that provides an effective mechanism to forecast and monitor all the components of the income account. The personal budget is a system that encourages people to change their perspective from just financial transactions processing to anticipating as well as managing the big picture of their income account. It is an important tool to get the best results from the income account mechanism.

Some people look at the income account as a backward looking document and prefer to concentrate more on the forward-thinking money management workouts such as personal budget. However, they often tend to disregard the fact that the personal budget merely adds planning aspects to the income account and both are important for efficient money management and are meant to reinforce as well as build on each other. Moreover, the first step in the dynamic process of establishing a useful personal budget is to analyze the income account so as to provide an authentic base to estimate the various components of the budget. In view of that, it is better to keep the format of the personal budget comparable to the income account as it is intended to forecast and monitor the same items.

There are many personal budget programs available in the market from both internationally reputed companies as well as local players catering to special market segments. But your self-designed program is likely to be an endearing as well as enduring one as it potentially renders better features. Your own budget template will be more flexible, user-friendly, time efficient and economical. It is always better to invest a little time in your own budget program.

You may consult some benchmarks to explore how much people spend in various expense categories, but you should be very careful about using this information to establish your budget. Only your income accounts can provide the most authentic pointers to develop your own personal budget. You cannot substitute experience with knowledge or technology here. Perfecting your budgeting exercise is a dynamic and an ongoing exercise. The following table shows the format of the personal budget, which is duly aligned with the summarized income account in order to harmonize both the processes.

Personal Budget Worksheet

Code	Monthly Total	Budgeted Amount	Actual Amount	Variation
I	Revenue Income			
	Expenses:-			
E.L.	Living			
E.D.	Personal Debt			
E.H.	Housing			
E.F.	Family Care			
E.T.	Transport			
E.R.	Recreational			
E.M.	Miscellaneous			
E.	Total Expenses			
I-E	Net Earnings Surplus/Deficit			
3	Returns Income			
3 + (I-E)	Long-Term Resources			

As is evident from the above table, the personal budget is simply a well thought-out forecast of our income, expenses and savings. This category wise forecast provides us a real sense of financial direction. It also encourages us to follow the requisite financial discipline that has the potential to make a real difference to our financial status. It empowers us to manage our money in such a way that helps us to maintain a reasonable standard of life as well as realize our financial goals. That is why the importance of budgeting in the routine money matters cannot be overstated.

Monitoring Cash Flows

Money flows in and flows out and at times, in unequal amounts. Monitoring cash flow is the ability to manage these flows to our advantage. The workings of the budgeting process also provide an insight on the likely cash flows during the period under review. This way it avoids the stress and edginess often induced by a sudden cash flow problem. Prior information helps us to deal with the deficit in a much better way. Similarly, advance information about surplus enables us to deploy these funds in a planned and profitable manner.

Since cash flow forecast presents an opportunity beforehand to create a clear-cut financial pathway for the present and future, it is advisable to make budget cum cash flow statement at least for the next quarter. Ideally, it should be forecasted month wise for the next year in advance. This can be done simply by incorporating columns for all the months in the personal budget worksheet. Cash flow deserves priority treatment, as it acquaints us in advance with the probable ripples and repercussions of our money maneuvers. And the cash flow cum financial budget is not just about control. In fact, this process seeks to optimize our actions and makes sure that we are in control of our money and using what we have to get what we truly want.

It is human nature to believe in our decisions. And we need our own mechanism to validate our decisions to ensure that our outlays fetch the desired outcomes. Our experience confirms that those who adapt an apt mechanism to monitor their spending habits and are well aware of the potential benefits of their mechanism consistently save more and spend less than those who adapt the mechanism but do not rightly appreciate the positive side effects. Simply thinking that you are following a good regimen can help you increase your potential gains.

Often preconceived notions result in 'spending vs. savings' debate, i.e., to spend more to live a comfortable life or save more for a bright future. One has to take a judicious call and balance these two considering all the relevant factors. While preferring one to another, take to heart that you are not denying yourself. Rather you are in favor of one option over another— expense A over expense B or savings over expense X. Remember you are the decision maker. And you are not restraining yourself rather you are opting for some options more than others. It is important to carry the right attitude. Bear in mind that you are sacrificing a less important urge for a potentially more rewarding experience.

Improving your financial fitness is a beginning without an end, as it continually encourages you to improve on your money management. Maintaining your enthusiasm over the long haul is the key to improve your success rate in the wealth creation endeavors. Your financial fitness regimen is about doing what is right for you, financially. It is about striking the right balance between spending and savings. And this makes your financial fitness format unique, as it depends on what befits your financial vision.

Part 3

The Science of Making Money

3.1 Understanding Investing: Making Money from Money

We all invest, financially and otherwise. The basic concept of investing is so simple and obvious that we often fail to appreciate what investing is. Investing is simply the proactive use of our resources. When we invest, we are putting something of ours into something else with the intent of achieving something bigger. In the financial context, investing is putting money in an endeavor with the expectation of profit, i.e. making more money. The intent in investing is to ensure that our money is also working hard to make more money for us with the aim of maximizing our overall earning potential. In simple terms, investing is the process of exploring what to do with our money and what the money can do for us. The idea is to upgrade our approach from savers to investors.

At this point, it is important to distinguish between Savings and Investing. Savings can be defined as the excess of income over expenditure. It is the accumulation of money set aside for future use. When money is astutely committed in order to generate more money, it becomes investment. Saving is a relatively passive activity wherein we set aside a definite amount of our earned income. Savings give more emphasis on security of capital and return expectations are secondary. Here the primary focus is on redirecting some money from our current income to actualize our future goals. On the other hand, investing is a dynamic activity wherein more emphasis is on the returns or profits. Investing calls for a proactive approach to make more money from the diligent use of money. It focuses on returns as well as associated risks and can navigate the spectrum from very aggressive to very conservative risk-rewards ratio.

Investing too conservatively can be as harmful as investing too aggressively. The science of investing empowers us to strike the right balance between cautious and aggressive approach while choosing various investments, such as shares, bonds, real estate, mutual funds, and so on.

Investing is for everyone, not just the rich. And the main risk many investors face is not educating themselves, assuming they are not rich enough to justify a wholehearted attempt. However, when they buy a cell phone, they spend days to check all the models, prices, features, and all that. But often that is not the case when it comes to investing their hard earned money. Success in today's competitive investment world depends on how one draws on her or his knowledge to make the right investment decisions. Moreover, the art of investing is slowly but surely evolving into the art as well as science of investing. The art of investing approach is more interested in insight, information and impulses. And the science of investing stresses on scrutiny, system and structure. But both lay emphasis on the latest knowledge. Investors need to adopt a workable approach to exploit the both in tandem to develop a systematic approach to investing.

Managing one's investments is becoming more and more complex and challenging due to rapidly growing investment avenues, which offer plethora of opportunities along with intrinsic risks. Managing your investments in such a scenario requires you to put in requisite efforts and stick to disciplined investing based on research and analysis so as to maximize your returns and minimize your risks. You have to appreciate how investing works in order to realize your investment goals. The dynamic world of investments and the uncertainties of future leave you with one thing you can always count on. That is your wisdom. You require knowledge, discipline and perseverance to win the investment game, and let your money work wonders for you. You can expect to get what you want from your investments only by taking an active stance in managing your investments. And you just need to have reasonable understanding of investments and a sound plan to realize your financial vision.

Key Factors to Successful Investing

The first step in investment planning is to acquire a clear understanding of various factors influencing investment decisions. This basic knowledge will not only empower you to create your best-fit investment portfolio, but also equip you to review it from time to time and realign it in the light of current situation in order to make efficient use of your capital. This knowledge will enable you to create a personalized investment plan, which will provide direction and momentum to your investment endeavors.

Now that we have a general idea of what investing is and why it is so vital to realize our financial vision, let us discuss some basic factors. These factors are prerequisites to successful investing, and you should wisely grasp them before investing. These will help you develop a realistic and balanced investment plan aimed at securing your financial future.

Define your Investment Objectives

The first and foremost step is to have a clear vision of your investment objectives. You should write down your specific investment goals along with justifications to have a clearer picture of what you need to do with your capital and incremental savings. Bear in mind that desires, which are inconsistent with your financial vision, cannot be your investment objectives. You have to invest your time and energy to finalize your specific investment goals depending on your personal circumstances because there cannot be a standard list of investment objectives for every individual. Being as clear-cut as feasible when finalizing your objectives will help you plan well and harmonize your investment portfolio to suit your stated goals. You get a good head start towards successful investing when you have a clear understanding of your objectives as well as underlying reasons.

Target Realistic Vision

It may not be very difficult for a veteran investor to follow a pragmatic approach and expect reasonable returns from investments. But some investors, particularly those new to investing, may have unrealistic expectations that are too high or too low. However, past trends coupled with future forecasts of any investment category can give a fairly accurate view of expected returns and associated risks to any investor, veteran or novice. Examining the history of any investment avenue can provide a sensible assessment of future rewards despite the fact that the past performance does not guarantee repeat performance. That is why they say, "It's hard to make predictions - especially about the future." But then, one can reasonably predict the probable future performance of any investment avenue based on average annual returns for a significant long period, and find out whether this is in harmony with her or his investment objectives.

The Human Factors

After knowledge, next important factor to determine your investment quotient is your emotional quotient. Mostly investment decisions are influenced by the human factors, predominantly greed and fear. Nine out of ten investors incur absolute or notional losses while succumbing to the personal pressures of greed, fear and hubris.

There is always a loser against every winner in the world of volatile investments. Invariably these losers are the victims of greed or fear. Irrational greed and fear can even hamper an investor's ability to take judicious investment decisions.

Many investors believe in the long term investing and resolutely invest for the long term, but fear factor grips them as and when their investments dwindle down by 10-20%. They get panicky and resort to panic selling. Many a times they buy the same instruments at 10-20% higher valuations and again pledge to stay invested for the long haul. On the other hand, many people are prone to close the eyes to the sunk costs in their bad investments. Such people have an aversion to accept losses. They throw more good money after bad investments in the name of averaging their acquisition costs. Their aversion for accepting losses tempts them to take increasingly bigger gambles in the hope of covering up their losses.

Impulsive and compulsive actions or reactions in the investment game are the other crucial hindrances to the successful investing. In this ever-changing world of investments, personal investment planning has to be a dynamic affair. But it does not mean that spur-of-the-moment decisions influence the investment strategy rather than well thought-out decisions that are in line with the long-term financial objectives. Therefore, it is imperative to keep your emotions in check to facilitate efficient wealth creation.

Risk- Return Ratio

The two main objectives of any investment are to maximize returns and minimize risks. In spite of that, most investors typically chase returns while they commit the cardinal sin of ignoring risks. They tend to forget that investments, which earn the highest returns, are also carrying the highest risks. Evaluating potential returns as well as intrinsic risks in any investment decision is the key to win the investing game. In view of the importance of returns and risks in the investment strategy, we intend to deal with these factors thoroughly in the next chapter.

Investment Tips

One has to absorb the media hype or investment advice from unreliable sources through the lens of rational wisdom in order to put such investment tips in the right perspective. The media hype can easily cloud the vision of people with 'quickly get rich' mindset and may lure them to speculate arbitrarily, contrary to their investment plans. Likewise, investment tips from the self-proclaimed advisors have the potential to jeopardize a well-organized investment plan. Such unauthentic information invariably leads to derailing the specific investment strategy resulting in non-fulfillment of desired financial objectives. Therefore, you have to bear in mind that what you do not know can harm you.

Reasons Not to Invest

One can point out several reasons to start investing. But there are just two valid reasons, which discourage investment. Lack of knowledge and debt are the two main grounds that can make one not to invest. And it is advisable not to invest until these stumbling blocks are removed. While there is no justification for the lack of basic knowledge, one can be favorably inclined to investing in the case of debt provided the assured rate of return on the investment is more than the interest outgo on the debt. However, it may not always be a valid justification to discount the importance of breaking the shackles of the debt trap. Besides, one should also appreciate that the investments that depreciate with time as well as do not generate returns are not investments in the true sense.

Speculation vs. Investment

One should make a clear distinction between speculation and investment. Speculation is the process of choosing high-risk investments in expectation of better rewards from anticipated price fluctuations. Casual investing is also termed as speculation. In our context, speculation is not an outright no-no as it is not always detrimental to our objectives. Speculation is different from gambling, which is based on random results. Here speculation implies that an investment risk can be reasonably assessed and analyzed. We are referring to the intelligent speculation within the defined parameters. And this has to be in agreement with the individual's investment profile. On the other hand, reckless speculation can be equated with gambling and hence is not desirable.

However, there is no harm in allocating a small part of your portfolio to speculative instruments provided you have the wherewithal to carry out the monitoring process diligently and open to seeking higher yields and greater risk.

Moreover, speculation is considered necessary for the efficient functioning of the world of investment as it provides much needed liquidity to the markets to facilitate active participation by investors, day-traders, hedgers and arbitrageurs. While speculators give up the safety of their capital in anticipation of higher returns, investors seek to preserve their capital as they get reasonable returns. It differs from investment primarily on account of degree of associated risk. With an eye to capitalize on market volatilities, even prudent investors often set aside a reasonable percentage of their capital, which is not earmarked to any important goal, to speculative instruments as a part of overall investment strategy. Speculation is essentially short term in nature and demands constant monitoring in a robotic way. Despite everything, it is usually better for busy professionals to opt for long-term investments rather than speculative instruments, particularly when the requisite time, temperament and talent are lacking.

Opportunity Cost of Capital

In simple terms, opportunity cost of capital is the reasonable rate of return that an investor would receive if the same capital were invested somewhere else with similar risk. It helps to quantify the difference in returns between a selected investment and one that is relinquished to pick the chosen investment. To say differently, it measures the gain/loss you could have received by taking an alternative investment. You should periodically figure out opportunity cost of capital from your perspective as well as market's view.

Over a period of time when you re-acquaint yourself with the available investment options and your changed circumstances, your investment logics are bound to change and so is your assessment of opportunity cost of capital. A good judgment of your opportunity cost makes you nimble-footed to capitalize on available opportunities, especially when your investment portfolio is flexible enough. Experts often suggest creating a long-term plan based on your personal financial goals and sticking to your plan for maximum gains. Nevertheless, it is equally important to appraise and adjust your portfolio on a regular basis to reconfirm whether your returns are in line with the contemporary market opportunities.

Asset Allocation

Asset allocation is the single most important factor to influence overall performance of your investment portfolio. It helps you to diversify your portfolio across various investments such as equity, bonds, real estate, commodities, cash and the rest. Asset allocation refers to choosing an optimum investment mix to achieve your desired financial goals. Asset allocation is a proven strategy to balance your portfolio in line with your overall investment planning. Asset allocation ascertains how much of each investment should be in your portfolio to optimize your overall investment earnings. It aims to lower investment risks while maximizing returns. However, it does not guarantee rewards or shield against investment risks.

Dr. Harry M. Markowitz discovered in 1952 that the right asset allocation is the most important factor in determining entire portfolio performance. He was awarded the Nobel Prize in 1990 for his work on efficient portfolio construction. Over the last many decades, we have seen that Dr. Harry's modern portfolio hypothesis withstood the test of time. The main lesson derived from his study is that determining assets mix among equity, bonds, commodities, real estate, etc. is the most important decision an investor makes, and this apparently simple process is the key to long-term investment success. He avers that right asset allocation is far more important than even the investments themselves and the time to buy or sell.

Without deliberating on somewhat obscure theoretical explanations supporting the supremacy of asset allocation in the investment decisions domain, we proceed to find out how you can choose an asset mix that is just right for you. Here you are supposed to decide what proportion of your portfolio you should allocate into equity, bonds, cash, real estate, etc. to realize your financial vision. It is not an easy exercise to formulate an optimum asset mix corresponding to your long-term and short-term financial goals.

It is important to understand that no standard formula can determine the right asset allocation for every individual. Since your investment objectives and conditions are unique, you need to customize your assets mix in harmony with your needs. Your best-fit asset allocation depends on your investment objectives, time horizons, knowledge, and risk tolerance. While deciding the right assets mix, you should also take into account your age, income, spending pattern, net worth, retirement plans, etc. Your financial objectives vary depending on your stage in life and so does your asset allocation. Experts normally recommend to invest only X percentage in volatile investments where X is equal to (100- your age). This may be a sensible approach for people looking forward to returns from their investments to provide for their post-working life.

It is desirable to review and adjust your assets mix periodically in an attempt to capitalize on contemporary investment opportunities as well as realign the portfolio in the light of latest asset prices. You need to change your asset allocation whenever there is a significant variation between the planned asset mix and actual asset mix. For example, if your planned allocation for equity is 35% but it has risen to 50% due to market appreciation, you are required to sell a part of equity to re-establish the equity share to 35%. In addition, you must re-examine your asset allocation whenever the variables determining your asset allocation change or you sense any significant change in your life or the investment climate.

To find the right asset allocation and deal with the rebalancing issue, there are various asset allocation strategies, such as strategic asset allocation, dynamic asset allocation and tactical asset allocation. Strategic asset allocation refers to an optimum buy and hold strategy wherein portfolio is adjusted periodically. As the name suggests, dynamic asset allocation emphasizes on continuous updating of asset allocation to capitalize on the market volatility. Third one i.e. tactical asset allocation is rather a mix of the previous two strategies. You may choose the one that suits your investment objectives as well as your profile as an investor.

For the sake of elucidation, here we depict a simple asset allocation table showing asset mix for a conservative and an aggressive investor. First, let us scan some important points relating to the assets allocation table.

> Real Estate investment is considered necessary in the form of a dwelling unit or investments clearly marked for a house. Percentage allocation for house varies significantly from person to person considering her/his unique circumstances. But then, the first house is a must. And it should be preferably kept out of the purview of the asset allocation metrics, especially in the case of middle-income people. For the sake of simplicity, we are assuming half the capital for this asset category and apportioning the balance half as 100% among other investment avenues.

> Conservative investors are risk-averse people, who are usually middle-aged investors, retirees or those nearing retirement.

> Aggressive investors are generally young people who seek higher returns and are prepared for higher risks.

> You should choose asset classes after understanding your risk-return profile and assessing your risk tolerance.

> Investments in equity or bonds can be executed through mutual fund and/or directly. However, mutual fund route is better for beginners.

> Asset percentages are given merely to exemplify the concept in simple terms and are not intended as investment advice since that calls for a unique investment strategy for every investor.

> You may adopt conservative or aggressive approach depending on your investment objectives. You may opt for a combination of these to suit your specific short-term and long-term goals.

> If you are approaching retirement and seeking a steady income from your nest egg in the near future, you have to adopt the conservative approach and allocate the requisite funds to fixed income securities. On the other hand, if your goal is wealth creation over a long haul, you should opt for an aggressive approach.

Asset Allocation Table

(Percentage)

Investment Type	Conservative Investor	Aggressive Investor
Real Estate/House	Yes	Yes
Equity-Growth:-		
Large Cap	10	20
Mid/Small Cap	5	10
Equity-Value:-		
Large Cap	15	25
Mid/Small Cap	5	10
Bonds	35	20
Other Fixed Income Investments	25	10
Cash/Cash equivalent	5	5

Creating your Investment Plan

Investment plan is a tool that provides you a structure to realize your investment objectives. It enables you to profit from the available investment options in a practical and objective manner. Your plan provides you the direction but requires you to put in the requisite efforts to actualize your financial vision. You have to follow the investment fundamentals as well as keep yourself abreast of the contemporary opportunities so as to succeed in the investment planning process. Here are the steps to judiciously develop and intelligently monitor your investment plan.

1. Define your Goals

As discussed earlier, the first step in creating your investment plan is to describe your important goals. These should be itemized as financial goals and committed to paper. It is advisable to classify your goals according to time horizon besides prioritizing them along the lines of your needs and wants. At this stage, you need to specify the time horizons as short term, medium term and long term where up to two years is short term, between two to seven years is medium term and more than seven years is long term. Clearly defining your goals will not only facilitates your investment process at every step but will also assist you to choose which investment avenues might be right to realize your specific goals. This will also give you a broad idea of future value of capital required and the time available to achieve every goal. Here is a hypothetical illustration.

Financial Goals Worksheet

Goals	Time horizon	Priority
Create a Contingency Fund	Short-Term	High
To Buy a House	Long-Term	High
Save for Child's education	Medium-Term	Medium
World Tour/Holidays	Not defined	Low
Buy a new Car	Short-Term	Medium
Savings for Retirement	Long-Term	High
Build Wealth	Long-Term	Medium

2. Understand your Investment Temperament

Your investment temperament has some bearing on all your investment decisions and as such influences the success potential of your investments. The legendary investor Warren Buffet avers that the single most important factor for investors is their 'temperament'. You have to ascertain your investment temperament so that you can devise a realistically compatible investment methodology. You should first explore your returns expectations in comparison with the markets outlook. Next, you need to determine your risk tolerance level as well as how you respond to the market volatility. You should also objectively determine whether you inherently prefer an aggressive approach or you trust a risk-averse passive approach. Before you finalize your plan, you should decide on the suitable investment approach that complements your emotional perspective towards every important goal.

3. Firm up Resources to Invest

In this step, you are supposed to determine your capital as well as other means to augment your investments. You are required to finalize your savings blueprint for the near term and forecast savings potential for the long-term. This will enable you to earmark your capital and future savings to the various goals. Your personal financial status and income account can readily provide you the relevant data.

4. Finalize Time Horizon

In the first step, you have determined the time horizon preferred by you to accomplish your investment goals. Now taking into account your resources, you need to specify precisely the time required to realize your objectives. Even though flexible approach is desirable at the execution stage, you should work out specific time period for every goal. For the long-term goals, it is advisable to note down the time span in preference to specific time.

5. Select Investment Vehicles

Next step is to explore the suitable investment avenues, which meet the above-mentioned criteria and have the potential to realize your goals. This is the time to give tentative shape to your asset allocation strategy. You must select only those investments, which you understand well. We will discuss the various investment vehicles in detail in the following chapters to enable you to reconsider and finalize your assets allocation strategy.

6. Review Performance

You must review the performance of your portfolio regularly to check if it is outperforming the market and other similar investment options. Periodically, it is also essential to check that notional or realized returns compare favorably against the expected returns. However, you need not review your long-term investments on a day-to-day basis since it can lead to impulsive inferences prompting you to take inept investment decisions. In the investment domain, the knee jerk reactions often trigger incorrect decisions. So, you should not allow short-term considerations to overwhelm your long-term game plan. On the other hand, you should suitably modify your investment portfolio whenever you find that the performance of your investment mix for a considerable period is not up to the mark as compared to your expectations or the chosen market benchmarks. And you are also supposed to adjust your portfolio whenever your investment objectives change.

At this stage, your investment plan may appear to be an intricate document, perhaps with some contradictions that can be addressed while finalizing it after appreciating all the aspects of investment planning.

Your investment plan depends on you, and you cannot blindly rely on external sources to take your investment decisions. Many unscrupulous investment advisors thrive by keeping investors in the dark about investing nitty-gritty. Their business model is built on investors' ignorance. So remember, you may not get the complete picture from your investment advisor, as she or he may perhaps like to skip some points that are counterproductive to her or his business interests. Moreover, they are generally better salespersons than investment advisors since their remuneration is often based on their volumes. This ubiquitous practice of rewarding investment professionals based on their business performance rather than their functional performance creates a conflict of interest, which is expectedly detrimental to investors' interests. No wonder these services are big business and are getting increasingly lucrative, often at the expense of naive investors. In short, it is always better to do some research before taking the investment advice of others at face value.

The next important point is that you must distinguish between investing and gambling. Investing is not gambling, but reckless investing can be termed as gambling. Genuine investing demands some action on your part and not just relying on luck to make bucks. Unlike gambling, investing demands perseverance and wisdom. In addition, you need to be wary of temptations, adhocism, and very short-term outlook. However, you should not always expect to win the investment game as no one can win this game consistently. What really matters in the ultimate analysis of this investment game is your success rate and the end result.

While the objective of an investment plan is to realize our financial vision, there are no straight answers to all investing questions. Generally, the answer lies in a mix of strategies geared to realize our investment goals. Investing is as much a tool for securing our financial future as it is for making the best use of our money for our loved ones and ourselves. Investing is what enables us to realize our financial vision. We can take charge of our destiny by taking charge of our investments.

3.2 Decoding the Risk-Return Paradigm

Investing is interesting, as it essentially seeks success. But our investments cannot afford the luxury of experimenting. Any investment intrinsically involves a variety of risks, and ignorance of these risks makes our investments vulnerable to losses. In the return-versus-risk tradeoff, most investors typically display a propensity to overlook risks in an attempt to enhance returns. On the other hand, some overcautious investors tend to close their eyes to the lucrative investment opportunities while seeking safety of their capital. Their aversion for risks tempts them to follow the ultraconservative approach, which may not fetch sufficient returns even to preserve the purchasing power of the principal. Success in investing depends on how one maximizes returns as well as mitigates risks.

The aim of investment planning is to attain the right balance between returns and risks. It calls for a rational approach to draw on the both to facilitate a judicious approach to investing corresponding to the individual's investment objectives. While the main criteria guiding our investment strategy is to get the best risk-adjusted returns, we should always bear in mind that more risk entails the greater potential for better returns or bigger losses from our investments.

As return and risk are the two most important and basic attributes for evaluating any investment, it is imperative to have a clear understanding of various types of returns and risks. This knowledge enables us to evaluate the efficiency of an investment or to compare the efficiency of several investments with an eye to create an efficient investment portfolio primarily catering to our financial needs and wants. In view of this, here we examine these two fundamental characteristics of any investment.

Higher Risk = Higher Potential Return

↑
R
e
t
u
r
n

Risk Premium

Risk-Free Return

Risk →

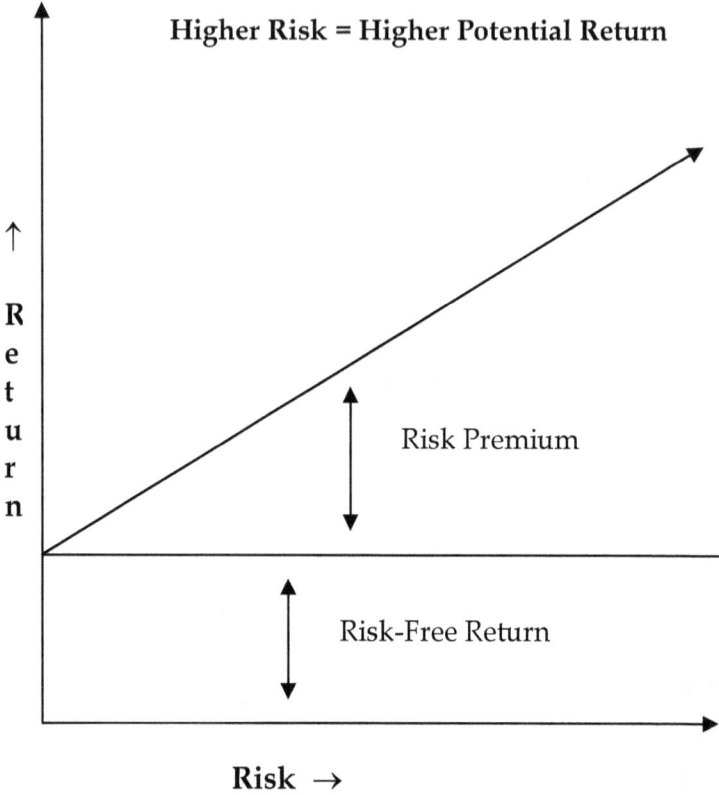

Investment Returns

Return on investment, also known as rate of return, rate of profit or sometimes just return, is the percentage change in value of the investment over a given period of time. Return on investment is a measure of the profit earned (or loss incurred) from each investment. It is the ratio of money gained or lost on an investment relative to the amount of money invested.

Return is the primary purpose of investing. It can be in the form of interest, dividend, capital appreciation or gain/loss. Well-informed investors often make more money during their lifetime from returns on their investments than from their occupation. People work hard to earn remuneration from their career but usually do not give due importance to their investment decisions which they tend to take too casually. Many such people deliver excellent achievements in their career but fall short in their personal investments. They usually deliver good results in their career because career life provides them a framework with enough checks and balances to ensure the output. This may not be the case with their investments since they are at liberty to invest in whatever way they like. The lack of discipline often makes them susceptible to disregard the basic investment principles.

What then is the way to inculcate the requisite self-discipline to upgrade our investment potential?

Fortunately, we just need to really recognize the importance and role of investments in our wealth creation endeavors to inculcate a habit of financial discipline.

Recognizing the importance of financial discipline encourages us to do our best to rationally take our investment decisions. Self-discipline makes it incumbent upon us to try our best to make sure that our investments also go all-out to deliver the right returns. So, it is desirable that we prudently devote some time to devise our investment strategy to target the right returns, which are consistent with our financial goals. We need to clearly understand and explore our suitable investment options in view of the fact that return needs vary from person to person as each individual is unique and so are her or his needs. In order to acquaint ourselves with the various attributes of returns, we need to explore different types of returns.

Absolute Return

Absolute Return is simply the gain or loss accrued on the investment and it consists of the income and/or capital appreciation. Return can be defined as the difference between accumulated balance of an investment and the principal invested. Here it is assumed that all distributions such as interest or dividend are reinvested. This is commonly known as the absolute return. The rate of return is calculated by dividing the absolute return by the principal amount to indicate investment profitability over a one-year period and as such is also known as annual rate of return. When the investment period is not one year, rate of return can be suitably adjusted to give a comparable one-year return, which is called annualized rate of return. Thus,

Absolute Return= accumulated balance of an investment – principal invested

Rate of Return in % = (Absolute Return ÷ principal invested) x 100

Real Rate of Return

Returns, even in percentage terms can be expressed in many ways and can have different implications. Investors need to figure out real rate of return to facilitate right comparison of various investment options on a standard scale.

For example, when you get 12% per annum return on an investment, it is a notional rate of return. You need to be concerned with real rate of return that can be calculated by adjusting notional rate of return with inflation and risk premium associated with the investment. When the expected inflation rate in your territory is 4% and the risk premium attached to the particular category of investment is 3%, your real rate of return will be 5%, which is calculated as follows.

Real rate of return = Notional rate – Inflation rate – Risk premium

Real rate of return = 12% - 4% -3% = 5 %

The notional rate of return is normally stipulated only for the fixed income investments. For other investments, one has to consider the expected rate of return to compute the real rate of return.

Inflation varies from country to country. But it remains theoretically the same for all investors in a particular economy. However, this may not be true since the impact of inflation on different individuals cannot be gauged with respect to national averages. Secondly, it is not possible to forecast the inflation accurately for the future period. Yet, it is advisable to consider estimated inflation rates for evaluating your real rate of return.

Risk premium also varies considerably from investment to investment. It can be taken as zero for investments where capital with returns is legally secured. On the other hand, risk premium can be considerably high for many volatile investments such as equity, artworks and commodities. But then, the return expectations from these investments are also equally high.

Effective Rate of Return

When returns are subjected to differential tax treatment, even the real rate of return may not be the right yardstick to evaluate your investment vehicles. You may have to adjust returns according to tax treatment of various investment avenues. Some investments may give you lower returns but offer tax exemptions or other benefits and, as such, may possibly result in higher yield. In such a case, your post tax return or the effective rate of return is the true yardstick to compare your investment returns.

Relative Rate of Return

Your investments are a part of the broader market and are influenced by it. This is why you ought to have the market returns as benchmark against which performance of your investments should be evaluated. When you calculate the above-mentioned rate of returns, you are simply calculating absolute returns paying no attention to the benchmark returns. You need to evaluate your returns vis-à-vis market returns of similar investments to carry out a comparative appraisal of your investments. Relative return is the difference between your return and the market return or benchmark return of the similar investments. In order to provide a meaningful analysis, the relative return takes into account not only your returns but also how the pertinent market indices are performing.

To further clarify this, suppose your equity portfolio has yielded 1% and 10% rate of return respectively in the last two years. Naturally, you would be quite pleased with 10% return of the previous year. But then, if your equity portfolio gives a return of 1% in a bearish market when relevant market index is down by 10%, it is a very good performance because just preserving your investments in a bearish phase is a big achievement. Similarly, if your equity portfolio appreciates by 10% in a bullish phase when market index has gone up by 20%, your performance is not good enough as it has yielded a negative relative return of ten percent (10%- 20%=-10%). This table shows the relevance of relative return.

Period	Absolute Return	Index Return	Relative Return
First Year	1	-10	11
Second Year	10	20	-10

For sound investment analysis, you should always consider the relative rate of return. It helps you to ascertain whether you or your fund manager is performing well or not. It provides you a standard yardstick to evaluate your investment strategy and respond appropriately when your portfolio is underperforming the market. If your investments are not yielding better than market returns, you will be better off by investing in index instruments where market returns are assured and transaction costs are minimal.

You are aware that return on investment can be calculated in many ways. Some unscrupulous people often manipulate the rate of return to suit their motives and misrepresent it to hoodwink gullible investors. One such common trick is misrepresenting factual return or interest as flat rate, or simple rate, or compound rate of return. You need to understand the distinction between these and preferably take your investment or borrowing decisions based on the real rate of return/interest.

Flat Rates — a Marketing Gimmick

Many people take loans because of an attractive flat rate considering it a wise step, especially when their investments are generating much better returns. With the intention of enticing innocent borrowers, scheming agents calculate flat rate linearly, rather than on a reducing balance method that take into account the repayments. Some experts say that the flat rate is roughly half the real rate of interest. However, it is a misconception, which is clear from the following table wherein flat rates vs. reducing balance rates are depicted.

Flat Interest Rate vs. Reducing Balance Rate

Flat Rates	Reducing	Balance	Rates - %
%	2Years	5Years	10Years
4	7.51	7.43	7.12
6	11.13	10.86	10.22
8	14.67	14.14	13.12
10	18.16	17.27	15.86
12	21.57	20.31	18.50

Flat rates are calculated based on original loan amount without subtracting principal repaid in successive installments, whereas in the case of reducing balance interest is charged based on how much of the original loan amount remains unpaid, which decreases as periodic installments are paid. That is why borrowing (or investment) decisions based on the flat rates invariably result in losses.

Compound Rate of Return

When you invest on the basis of compound rate of return, the return earned is reinvested and it becomes the capital yielding the same rate of return in future. It increases the annual yield because returns reinvested as capital also yield returns. Even at moderate rate of returns, investors can multiply their money over long periods due to the time value of money and power of compounding. Let us exemplify the impact of simple and compound rate of return with the help of a simple example.

If you invest $100 at 10% simple rate of return or interest, you get $10 every year as your return. When your rate of return is simple rate of return, i.e., returns are not reinvested, your total capital including returns will be $200 in ten years, $300 in twenty years and $400 in thirty years.

If you invest the same amount of $100 @ 10% compound rate of return, your total returns will be substantially higher as is clear from the following table, which shows that your total proceeds will be $259 in ten years, $673 in twenty years and $1745 in thirty years. It can be presented as return of 159 % in ten years, 573 % in twenty years and 1645 % in thirty years, or annualized return at the rate of 15.9% (159 divided by 10), 28.7% (573 divided by 20) and 54.8% (1645 divided by 30) respectively.

These returns are significantly higher due to the power of compounding. Long-term investors can expect progressively better returns with each passing year. The real impact of compounding becomes evident if you consider what happens when the returns are not reinvested.

Power of Compounding

(Figures in $)

Year	Capital at the beginning	Return for the year @10%	Capital at the year end
1	100	10	110
2	110	11	121
3	121	12	133
4	133	13	146
5	146	15	161
6	161	16	177
7	177	18	195
8	195	19	214
9	214	21	236
10	236	24	**259**
...	...	...	...
20	612	61	**673**
...	...	...	...
30	1586	159	**1745**

You can take advantage of power of compounding and time value of money to secure your financial future and provide for long term goals like children's education and retirement. A small investment for the future of your little kid can provide her/him huge sums in future when she/he needs money. Small amount can multiply with the power of compounding over a long period. The following table depicts the impact of compounded returns at various rates of interest by exhibiting the accumulated balance at various age points on a small capital of $100 invested when the age of your child is 10 years.

Future Value of $100 at Different Interest Rates
(Figures in $)

Interest→ ↓ Age	5%	10%	15%	20%
10	100	100	100	100
20	163	259	405	619
30	265	673	1637	3834
40	432	1745	6621	23738
50	704	4526	26786	146977
60	1147	11739	108366	910044
70	1868	30448	438400	5634751

The Thumb Rule of 72

You can use the rule of 72 to calculate roughly the period that is required to double your investment at a particular compound rate of return. You just need to divide 72 by the rate of return to get a fairly accurate idea of years it will take to double your money. For instance, at 12 % rate of return, it will take 6 years to grow your capital to twofold and at 24%, it will take just 3 years to double up your capital.

Years needed to double the capital = 72 ÷ compound rate of return

Regular Returns vs. Capital Appreciation

Risk-averse investors typically invest in regular income yielding investments such as bonds, bank deposits and other interest-bearing instruments. These are good investment vehicles for passive and income oriented investors. However, investors need to consider the real or effective rate of return and the effect of compounding before investing so as to take care of the time value of money, their regular needs and long term objectives. Long-term historical averages suggest that one can expect 4-5 % return from regular income yielding investments.

Since fixed return investments often provide a low return, your capital may not be able to keep pace with the inflation. In fact, sometimes you may be actually eating into the purchasing power of your capital by investing in these instruments. You can manage this situation by investing in such investments which provide capital appreciation to counter the impact of inflation. Investments in shares, mutual funds, commodities, real estate and the like can offer you capital gain or loss. Generally, experts consider these investments as high-risk high-return investments, and as such, you need to research well and bear in mind the consequences of price volatility before committing. However, historical long-term performance is greatly in favor of these investments. For instance, shares have returned more than double the return of fixed income products in the last century. The same is the case with most of mutual funds, real estate and commodities. Furthermore, the long-term trend is of increasing average returns in these volatile investments. Worth of these investments fluctuates constantly and as such necessitates an active investment approach to maximize the gains or minimize the losses. Returns for these investments are normally computed with reference to capital appreciation and all the earnings received during the holding period of the investment.

Holding Period Return

Returns on equity or stocks are usually calculated for the holding period such as one year or five years. While calculating the holding period return, all the returns during that period including dividends, bonus, capital appreciation/depreciation, etc. are considered. The holding period return is calculated as follows:

Holding Period Return $= [dividends, interest, bonus etc. + (period end price – investment price)]

Holding Period Return % = [Holding Period Return ÷ investment price] x 100

The holding period return is illustrated in the following table. For the sake of simplicity, we are assuming that a share was purchased @ $100 (face value $10) at the beginning of the period and was sold at the end of five years @ $180. Company also paid dividend at the rate of 20 % every year. We are not considering income tax factor in the following calculation.

Calculating Holding Period Return of Stocks

↓Particulars\Year→	1	2	3	4	5
Purchase Price $	100				
Dividend %	20	20	20	20	20
Dividend $	2	2	2	2	2
Share Price $	110	105	125	155	180
Annual Return $	12	-3	22	22	27
Annual Rate of Return- %	12	-3	21	18	17
Holding Period Return - $					90
Holding Period Return - %					90%

It is relevant to note that the sum of annual rate of return for five years is significantly less than the holding period return owing to the power of compounding. It is also interesting to note that while dividend declared by the company is 20% but actual yield is far less, i.e., 2% (2 ÷ 100) for the first year and 1.29% (2 ÷ 155) for the fifth year. Company declares dividend on the face value of a share whereas actual yield to the investor is on his purchase price. When you buy a share at a premium to face value, your dividend yield will be less than the declared dividend rate. Conversely, if you buy equity at a discount to the face value, your yield will be more than the dividend rate. You should consider dividend yield and not the dividend rate while investing in equity with the aim of regular returns.

Investment Risks

People clamor for ideal investments. They want highly rewarding and risk free investments. But, just as in the real world, we cannot find an ideal job or an ideal spouse, similarly, we cannot find an ideal, risk-free investment. However, we can always manage risk in our investments as we manage our job and spouse. In fact, risk is all-pervasive, and there is no investment that is risk free. So, rather than seeking the elusive Holy Grail of investments, we should understand investment risk and use it to our advantage, as we do with our job and our spouse.

Risk is an integral part of investing. Risk is inseparable from return. It is important to understand risk, return, and the inevitable trade-off between the two. Appreciating the risk to return ratio is the key to successful investing. It may be true that the more risk you take the more returns you get. Long-term historical data substantiates this perception that greater risks yield greater returns. But here greater risk does not mean ignoring investment risks. Ignorance of risks in the investing world is a financial hara-kiri.

Innumerable people lose their returns and in some cases capital also by indulging in reckless investing without understanding risks. On the other hand, many people make fortune by taking well thought-out risks on their investments. People often wonder why the outcome is so widely divergent. It is so because winners are alert to risks and appreciate the risk-return paradox whereas losers have a tendency to focus on returns and in the process become oblivious to the intrinsic risks in their investments. Therefore, one needs to understand the risks of the investment world before finalizing investment strategy.

You cannot totally evade risks associated with the various types of investments. But you can judiciously manage your investment risks keeping in view your investment objectives. So, it is important that you enter any investment only after familiarizing yourself with the probable risks in an attempt to aptly harmonize your returns expectations with the likely risks. All investments have some sort of risk associated with them and each of these is of a different nature. Here we discuss some of the common investment risks with a view to put our risk perceptions in proper perspectives.

Financial Risk

Financial risk or default risk refers to non-realization of returns and/or principal invested. While investing, this is the first risk that springs to mind. This risk is more common in unsecured fixed return securities. However, one has the risk of squandering capital in equity, commodities and other volatile investments if one ventures without researching the prospect of the investment.

Interest Rate Risk

Fluctuations in interest rates can influence your investments. For example, any increase in interest rates will result in erosion of bond prices and vice versa. It can also affect prices of equity, commodities and other speculative investments since increasing interest rates are likely to result in diversion of funds from these investments to fixed income investments thereby softening the prices of these investments owing to tapering of demand. Small fluctuations in interest rates can trigger significant movement in prices of many investments. Interest rate increases also impacts profitability of businesses wherever interest is a significant component of revenues. Consequently, this leads to value erosion in the equity as well as other investments in these businesses.

Inflation Risk

Swinging inflation can influence investments in several ways. Most important yet often overlooked is the erosion in the value of purchasing power of your investments. Suppose you are getting good assured returns on your investment. Yet after the tenure of your investment if the purchasing power of accumulated balance of your investment is less than what it was when the investment was made, your factual return is negative. Reasonable inflation is considered healthy for the economy but unreasonable or negative inflation can play havoc with the economy as well as your investment strategy. Inflation influences many businesses in a negative or positive way. Suppose you sense that steel demand is likely to be robust in future and as such, steel prices can go up. In view of that, you invest in the equity of steel producing companies or in the steel as a commodity. You are likely to reap rich dividends in case steel prices indeed go up. Conversely, price of steel going down is a big risk that can cause substantial losses to your investments. Similarly, any business using steel as input or raw material is likely to suffer lower profitability owing to inflation in steel prices if it cannot pass on the entire inflation impact to its consumers.

Liquidity Risk

Liquidity implies investments can be promptly converted to cash or cash equivalents. This risk is the probability of loss in value that an investment will suffer when sold, i.e., converted to cash. Some investments necessitate relinquishing a part of return or principal so as to persuade somebody to buy. While liquidity risk is more relevant for retail and small investors, large investors are more cautious about it. Most investments are quite easy to sell, and as such, do not carry any significant liquidity risk premium. On the other hand, some bonds and money market instruments may only be redeemable at the end of their fixed term. These investments are not so liquid and can be sold only at a discount.

Business Risk

Business risk refers to poor management of company's operation that can adversely affect profitability of the business. Several factors such as poor management, outdated products, consumer unfriendly policies and technological obsolescence can harm the business of the company resulting in value erosion of its equity as well as all other securities issued by it.

Tax Risk

Tax risk refers to changes in the tax policies that can adversely affect your potential returns. For example, tax incentives on certain investments can be withdrawn before you cash in returns to avail predefined tax benefits. Similarly new taxes can be imposed on your investment before the tenure of your investment ends.

Industry Risk

Profitability potential or performance of an industry has a direct bearing on the prospects of investments made by several stakeholders in that industry. Poor performance of an industry can significantly affect investments in equity as well as other financial products of that industry. Continued poor functioning can trigger defaults even on fixed return instruments issued by the industry players. Many prudent investors enter into an industry at the time of its cyclical uptrend and exit when they sense the initial indications of the industry's downtrend thereby maximizing returns and minimizing risks.

Economy Risk

Status of economy influences the performance of various investments in that economy. When economy is worsening, there is considerable risk not only in volatile investments such as equity, commodities and real estate but also in relatively safer fixed return investment avenues to some extent. In contrast, in case of booming economy, one can expect excellent returns from non-fixed return investments. Global economic factors can also affect investments which are susceptible to the interplay of international factors. Generally, economic risk factors have more impact on high return kind of investments.

Country Risk

Country risk is specific to investments relating to that country or sometimes its neighbors. Country specific factors like geo-political tensions, political instability, economic crisis, prohibitive business regulations, unreasonable taxes, weak legal system and the rest can have an adverse impact on investments in that country.

Currency Risk

The performance of a country's currency vis-à-vis other major international currencies can affect not only economy of the country but also internal and international investments. Currency risk is the risk of an investment's value changing due to changes in currency exchange rates. It arises from exchange rate movements between pairs of currencies. International investments suffer adversely when the currency of the country strengthens. Conversely, international investments are likely to do well when the local currency depreciates. Fluctuations in currency rates vis-à-vis other major currencies also influence fortunes of domestic businesses dependent on international trade. Depreciating currency erodes the purchasing power of importers, and exporters suffer if currency appreciates.

Market Risk

Market Risk is the probability that the whole market will depreciate. It is often triggered by the external factors such as wars, drought, floods, bullish or bearish phases and so on. Market risk usually affects most of the investments. We should bear in mind that markets move in cycles. Markets go up, come down, go up... and this never-ending cycle goes on endlessly. So far, no theory or formula could explain the exact rational behind market's bullish or bearish phases or the duration of such phases. Experts attempt to forecast market movements based on technical analysis of historical data but the findings were never very correct.

Event Risk

Unforeseen events, such as Gulf war, 9/11 terrorist attack in the USA and 2008 mortgage crisis can impulsively suck the life out of the market investments. Event risks are unexpected, external and largely uncontrollable. Event risk can also be classified as market risk. At times, such events provide good opportunities to a select few investors who are carrying investments in commodities like gold and crude oil, which invariably flare up on such happenings. Similarly, speculators who are bearish on the market, and as such, carrying short positions make hay on such knee-jerk reactions. However, lately market movements are showing a mature behavior in the aftermath of such happenings. Nevertheless, such negative events pose a serious threat to the humanity as well as to most of the investors and dampen the economic climate to some extent.

Personal Risk

This is the most important category of investment risks because investors often gamble away their returns as well as their capital in many cases owing to their personal weaknesses. We regularly chance upon people who invest for the long term but get panicky if their equity or other volatile investments correct by just a few percentage points and resort to panic selling. Many a times they again buy the same investments at much higher prices, again swearing to invest for the long term. On the other hand, there are indolent investors, who are driven hither and thither by their volatile and wavering mind, which vacillates, unable to establish itself on any decision or action. The idea is not to discourage active monitoring of the portfolio but to avoid reckless actions, which often emanate from impulsive reactions to market movements as well as to encourage investors to proactively deal with procrastination, which often leads to missed opportunities. The objective is to encourage well thought out actions within a framework to eliminate or minimize the human factors that impetuously trigger wrong actions or lead to missed investment opportunities. These risks are easily controllable to a certain extent with right attitude and approach. Some pointers are given here to make you receptive to the personal factors, which have great potential to influence your investment quotient.

✓ Knowledge of your investments is an essential prerequisite to investing.
✓ Set realistic goals and adapt a flexible approach to your investment decisions. But beware of knee-jerk reactions.
✓ Determine your preferred comfort level in order to establish the optimum risk-return tradeoff.
✓ Right Temperament is the key to profit from volatile and high return investments.
✓ Irrational greediness and illogical fears often results in losing money.
✓ Be wary of buying or selling the right investments at the wrong time.
✓ Identify your bad investments in time to avoid extending your losses while holding on to such investments.
✓ Know your personal profile as an investor and harmonize your investments with it.

There are many risks for the investors, and there is no reliable method to avoid all the risks. Yet, understanding the investment risks need not persuade you against investing or coerce you to put your investment decisions on the back burner. We intend to encourage you to take charge of your investing process in a well-informed manner. This will facilitate you to take calculated and judicious risks with an eye to better returns. But you have to spend some time and effort in examining the risks associated with your intended investments so as to explore whether you are comfortable with these risks.

Risk Minimization Techniques

Since investment risks cannot be completely done away with, investors need to work towards managing these. Investors should assess their risk tolerance considering their objectives, financial position, investment horizon and comfort levels so that they can adapt risk minimization techniques accordingly. Investors have to keep in mind that generally lowering the risk entails lower returns. Risk minimization does not simply imply lowering the risks. It is all about managing the risks in accordance with the investor's profile. There are several techniques, which can be employed to manage investment risks effectively.

Diversification

The saying, "don't put all your eggs in one basket" is really meaningful when it comes to investing. It rightly emphasizes the importance of diversification to deal with investment risks. You can minimize your investment risks by spreading your investments across various asset classes, which have negative correlation. In simple terms, your portfolio should have a variety of securities, which move like a sea-saw. This is to ensure that your portfolio is always balanced in terms of risk- return quotient. By putting your money in a wide variety of investment avenues, you can minimize overall risk on your investment portfolio, even though all the investments separately may be carrying higher risks. This not only ensures lower risk in the overall portfolio but also assures higher returns on the specific investments. However, you should avoid overdoing diversification since a large portfolio carries the risk of deficient monitoring.

Long-Term Investing

A long-term outlook minimizes the risks inherent in investments yielding high returns. Historical data suggests that even highly volatile investments such as equity, real estate and commodities invariably provide quite good returns in the long term. Whenever your time horizon is long enough, you may well consider investing in high-return high-risk kind of securities where returns are generally higher with reasonable risks, which again tend to taper off with time. You can consider investing only that part of your portfolio in high-risk investments that is decidedly not required for specific purposes in the near future. However, long term investing is not a guaranteed antidote to investment risks because many a times investments that were not risky earlier become risky later since we live in a volatile world of investments.

Know your Investments

When you have a handle on your investments as well as your investment objectives, you are in a good position to handle your

Risk/Return Trade-Off of Common Investments

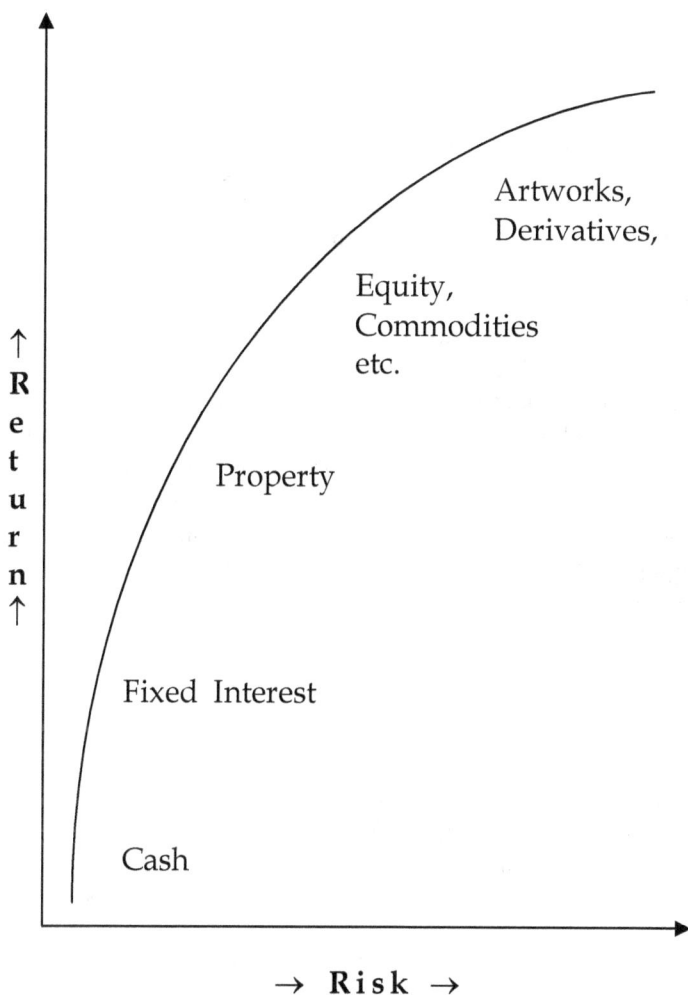

Artworks,
Derivatives,

Equity,
Commodities
etc.

Property

↑
R
e
t
u
r
n
↑

Fixed Interest

Cash

→ **Risk** →

risks effectively and responsively. The knowledge of investment
products and market movements enables you to identify the
potential winners and losers promptly. This in turn prompts you
to take timely action to accomplish your goals as and when
opportunity strikes. When you shift your money from likely
laggards to prospective leaders, you are reducing the investment
risks. Secondly, the market knowledge facilitates cashing

investments where targets are achieved. By realizing your goals before time, you not only preempt the investment risk but also get a chance to earn additional returns. For example, you have invested a part of your portfolio in equity investments with an eye to double the amount in five years so as to purchase a house. In case your equity investments increase to twofold in three years, you should convert, if not fully at least half, to money market instruments since precisely timing the market as per your needs is fraught with risks. This opportunistic withdrawal is essentially a goal-centric technique of risk minimization.

Hedging

Another risk reduction technique is hedging wherein you invest in another investment that cancels out the price fluctuation risk of your investment. Derivatives are market-created financial products used for hedging. A derivative is simply a contract between two parties relating to a certain underlying asset. Futures and options are the most common derivative instruments, which can be used for hedging investment risks in various asset classes. Hedging is more of a risk management tool as it also restricts the returns while reducing risks.

SIP and OWM

Systematic Investment Plan (SIP) means continuous investment of a fixed amount at regular intervals. It minimizes market-timing risk because you invest the same amount every time without considering price fluctuations. This facilitates cost averaging of securities to long-term investors, as they will get more units in a declining market and fewer units in a booming market. However, this plan does not shield you from losses in market corrections.

Opportunistic Withdrawal Method (OWM) requires you to keep an eye on the market movements and whenever market level crosses your targeted return level, withdraw a predetermined fraction of your investments. You may prefer to keep the proceeds in fixed return securities until you get an opportunity to invest again at lower levels to maximize your overall gains while minimizing your stakes. Here opportunistic withdrawal is primarily a profit maximization strategy indirectly geared to reduce the risk. Volatile investments such as equity, mutual funds, commodities and the like provide random opportunities to take such opportunistic advantage of your investments. As a risk minimization strategy, we have been advising this method particularly in equity index instruments for nearly three decades. Largely the success rates of this strategy are much better than simple invest-and-hold strategy. It came through well even when markets experienced event or other risks including the tech meltdown at the turn of 20th century or the 9/11 incidence near the financial hub of this world. However, we could not fully exploit the markets rise of 2007-8 as we failed to predict the abnormal rise during this period. As a result, we gradually shifted major chunk of the volatile investments covered by this strategy to fixed return instruments as mandated by this method. Therefore, even the opportunistic withdrawal method cannot always maximize your profits but it can somewhat shield you from severe market corrections and generate the best returns when the markets are range bound or direction-less.

Identify your Risk-Return Equilibrium

Return is a function of risk, and as such, you have to determine how much risk you can endure in your endearing returns endeavor. You have to be conscious to the fact that the more risk you take, the greater is the potential for higher returns or losses. So, with a view to ensure optimum returns, you should figure out your risk-return equilibrium, which is simply your comfort level of risk return tradeoff. Knowing your risk-return equilibrium will enable you to choose the right investments along the lines of your returns expectations and risk tolerance.

Risk taking potential varies from person to person as well as during the lifespan of an individual. At various stages in your life, your financial needs vary thereby prompting you to change your risk-return balance accordingly. You must keep an eye on this delicate balance throughout your investing life. The basic rule is that the lower the age, the higher the risk taking abilities and vice versa. In the early stages of career, you can afford to take more risks in anticipation of better returns, which befits that stage to accomplish the long-term wealth creation objectives. But you should adopt a middle-of-the-road approach during middle age that should give way to a more guarded approach in the last stage of your career. The idea is to invest savings in such a way that balance gradually shifts towards more reliable fixed return products over a period of time. This conventional model has withstood the test of time and has become the unquestionable standard for most of the employed people because it creates an optimal balance between wealth creation and securing financial future. The following diagram illustrates a basic model depicting risk return equilibrium at various life stages.

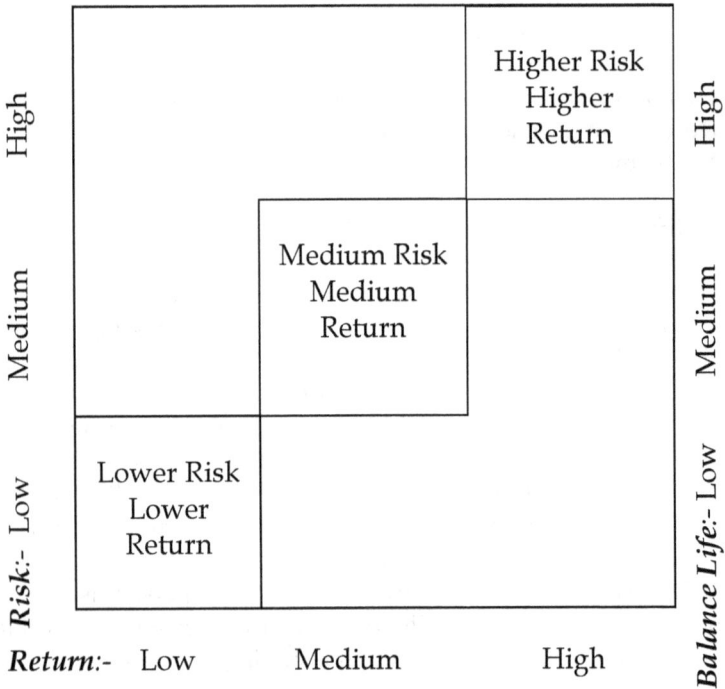

Risk-Return Equilibrium at Various Life Stages

			Higher Risk Higher Return	
		Medium Risk Medium Return		
	Lower Risk Lower Return			

Risk:- Low / Medium / High (vertical left axis)

Balance Life:- Low / Medium / High (vertical right axis)

Return:-   Low   Medium   High

Although the above time-tested model is suitable for most investors, it is not restrictive in scope. It is not meant to restrain everyone to follow this textbook model of risk return equilibrium. Any person with reasonable knowledge and shrewd approach to investing can choose her or his comfort level in the risk-return matrix notwithstanding the prescribed standards. Investors who are flush with funds can also choose their own risk return equilibrium at a higher or lower level. The fourth dimension of risk-returns matrix empowers you to select your own comfort area based on your investor profile overriding the standard levels usually prescribed based on the residual age considerations. In a nutshell, you may reposition your risk-return equilibrium as determined by your specific circumstances. The following diagram depicts how investor profile can prevail over the third dimension of age, which is traditionally responsible for determining the risk return balance.

Risk-Return Equilibrium- The Knowledge Effect

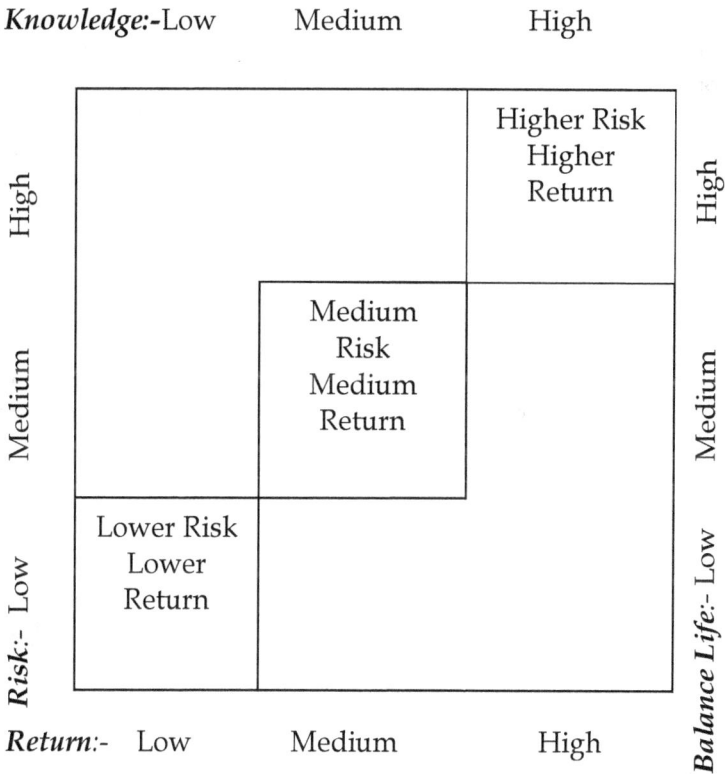

*Knowledge:-*Low   Medium   High

		Higher Risk Higher Return
	Medium Risk Medium Return	
Lower Risk Lower Return		

High   *Medium*   *Low*   (Risk:- Low)

High   *Medium*   *Low*   (Balance Life:- Low)

Return:- Low   Medium   High

Investors, who are reasonably proficient in the game of investing, may choose medium risk- medium return equilibrium even if their age mandates them to low risk- low return quadrangle. Further, they can use their expertise to maximize returns and minimize risks thereby repositioning their risk-return equilibrium at the right-top area of the applicable quadrangle. People invariably take advantage of assets allocation scheme to align their risk-return equilibrium at the desired position. Well-informed investors also draw on the concept of an efficient portfolio to maximize their returns for a given level of risk. In addition, successful investors are equally responsive to other factors touching on their investment returns and risks. In fact, decoding risk return paradox is all about establishing the right equilibrium in tandem with other risk minimization and return maximization strategies. However, establishing your risk-return balance is not a one off exercise. Perfect balance cannot be formulated over night, as it demands time, knowledge and experience.

Understanding and managing your risk return paradox is crucial to thrive in your wealth creation endeavors. But this seemingly simple contradiction has no sure-fire solutions. No one can unerringly manage risks on a consistent basis or expect absolute success in returns endeavors. It is an ongoing process, and you can definitely improve your risk return relationship. Out of the multitude of investment avenues, only knowledge will facilitate you to pick your portfolio that is compatible with your financial goals as well as harmoniously aligned with your risk/return trade-off. This wisdom will not only give you better returns but also enhance your risk management skills in other areas of life.

3.3 The Investing Universe: Understanding Asset Classes

Investment options are increasing in numbers. And they are becoming increasingly complex for a naïve investor. A few decades ago, investors used to clamor for varied and innovative investment options, and choosing the right product was an exciting experience. But due to the overabundance of investment options, nowadays perplexity has supplanted that penchant for more and better investment products. Besides, the sheer variety of investments with varying degree of risk-return quotient has made the process of picking the right investments really challenging, especially for the do-it-yourself kind of investors. That is why now retail investors consider the investment selection process a daunting exercise. But then, well-informed investors can devise their own process to profit from the problem of 'too many and too complex' investment alternatives. So, with a view to manage this superfluity to your advantage and gain from the plethora of investment options, you just need to follow a rational investment selection system to succeed in your wealth creation endeavors.

But the first and foremost hurdle is that most individual investors are not willing to spend the requisite time on their money management endeavors, especially the investment analysis part. They spend more time on choosing what to wear than choosing the right investments to park their capital. We know that looking good is important. And for some looking good is more important than feeling good. As Oscar Wilde rightly said, "Looking good and dressing well is a necessity. Having a purpose in life is not."

Rightly choosing our investments is not only important to survive in this inflationary world, but is a necessity to thrive in this materialistic world. In spite of this, procrastination often comes in the way of investing. Some investors take a laid-back approach to investing, taking the view that investing is a passive activity because it is contingent on luck. Yes, success in investing is contingent on a bit of luck, but luck is useless without a positive, proactive attitude. Due to a casual approach and tendency to take money matters lightly, many well-informed investors fail to apply their wisdom to multiply their capital. They fail to acknowledge that bulk of wealth is created through investments, including investments in entrepreneurship. On the other hand, many people habitually pay a hefty price for accumulating capital mainly through their occupation, as they often give up their leisure pursuits and sacrifice many other personal desires in their quest for wealth, which they strive to accumulate by working hard.

We all know that our ability to earn is our greatest asset. That is why investment in entrepreneurship offers the best returns. Here value addition in terms of entrepreneur's knowledge and efforts makes all the difference. This value addition is also relevant to investing because it can make sure that our money is working harder to make more money. But we should be willing and able to profit from it. So first, we need to assign the time and efforts we are willing to devote to pursue our investment goals. When we are inclined to invest our time and money within a defined framework, we are positively heading for success in our investment endeavors, i.e., we are taking a short cut to wealth creation.

The basics discussed in the previous chapters empower you to invest diligently your resources to realize your investment objectives. However, it is also equally important to ensure that you enter any investment with a clear understanding of the chosen investment as well as how it relates to your goals as stated in your financial plan. Therefore, before committing, you must understand the investments you choose for your portfolio and how these would serve your investment objectives. You should begin with the end in mind.

Before we take up the main points relating to various asset classes, we intend to revisit the leading factors that influence investment decisions. The objective is to incorporate some key factors in devising a simplified structure to assist you to choose your portfolio that match your needs. This will enable you to intelligently select investments, which are compatible with your investment plan.

Nearly all fundamental and important factors that should be evaluated to make a personal investment decision can be broadly classified into two categories, namely, Investment Criteria and Personal Criteria. Investment criteria cover factors specific to the investment option under consideration whereas personal criteria include individual factors of the investor. The following five fundamental factors from each category can help you set up a simple and standard framework to rationally evaluate various asset classes.

A. Investment Criteria
✓ Risk
✓ Income
✓ Capital Appreciation
✓ Volatility
✓ Liquidity
B. Personal Criteria
✓ Goals
✓ Knowledge
✓ Temperament
✓ Time horizon
✓ Asset allocation

How you invest your money is your own business. It is your personal issue. Similarly, the system that works best for analyzing your probable investments should also be personalized enough to provide for all your personal issues. The above framework fulfills the requirements of most people; however, you may well prefer to tweak it suitably to make it more responsive to your personal issues. Before we proceed further to discuss various asset classes, it is important to put in place the following disclaimer to put the general discussion in proper perspective.

Disclaimer: Since there cannot be any infallible yardstick for numerous investment options, this attempt to provide general information in a short and snappy way is designed to facilitate a broad review of common investment avenues for an uninitiated investor. The information provided in this book is intended to act as a general guide, and inexpert readers are advised to seek appropriate advice from qualified professionals before acting on any recommendation.

Equity Investment

Equity investment is the financial product of choice for millions of investors. This alluring investment avenue is often perceived as a primary investment category, especially by such investors who subscribe to the view that investment in financial instruments should only be considered for portfolio analysis. However, this is not factually true. Ideally, most of the asset classes should find a reasonable place in an investor's portfolio. Here it is important to note that equity investments are only a small part of total savings plowed into the financial instruments. In spite of everything, equity is one of the most important investment categories from the angle of long-term wealth creation. It has consistently returned superior long-term returns than any other financial product. The words equity, stocks and shares are synonymous for our purposes.

Shares represent the ownership interest in a company. That is to say, when you own shares, you really own a part of the company and have a claim on the company's profits when they are paid out in the form of dividends, etc. The intrinsic value of a stock is derived from the net worth of the company. It can be easily calculated by dividing the net worth with the number of outstanding equity shares. It is invariably different from the face value, which is not a significant indicator. However, the relevant value for an investor is the market price, which is determined by the market forces, i.e., demand & supply.

While equity investments are labeled as the best form of long-term investments, the inherent risks and volatility are sure to baffle many lay investors. Equity is a very volatile investment with a long-term upward tendency. The positive aspect of this volatility is the potential for better returns for an earnest investor. Yet, it can be quite risky for an uninitiated investor, especially in the short term. But the long term perspective radically changes the risk perception of equity, as evidenced by a remarkable performance in the last two centuries. This is despite the radical economic, political and social changes during this period. Further, various types of shares may perhaps give paradoxical returns. Which is why experts suggest the percentage of equity component in your financial portfolio should be 100 minus your age. So, at the age of 25, you should be 75% invested in equities and at the age of 65, 35% of your portfolio should be in equities. In other words, investment in equity should be a decreasing function of your age, as is depicted in the following table.

Calculating the Equity Component of Your Portfolio

Investor's Age	100 - Age	% of Financial Investments	
		Equity	Debt
25	75	75	25
35	65	65	35
45	55	55	45
55	45	45	55
65	35	35	65

Generally, shares are classified into large cap, mid cap and small cap based on the market capitalization, i.e., size of the companies. Market capitalization refers to the company's net worth based on the market price of the stock. It can be easily calculated by multiplying the market price of a share by the number of outstanding equity shares. Investment experts suggest balanced investments in large-cap, mid-cap and small-cap stocks so as to maintain a diversified allocation compatible with the investor's risk profile.

In addition, stocks are also classified as value oriented and growth-oriented stocks. Value investing reckons that company's balance sheet and other quantitative data provides enough indicators to select the right stock. Fundamental analysis is the spinal cord of value-oriented approach. It seeks out positive pointers, such as low price-to earning ratio, low debt-equity ratio, low price-book value ratio, high sales-market capitalization ratio, consistent profit growth, uninterrupted and decent dividend payouts and so on. Here the objective is to identify stocks that are available in the market at below the intrinsic value. On the other hand, growth oriented approach primarily looks for signs of above-average growth. Growth investing aims to buy stocks of growing companies and let the investments grow as the companies grow. It looks for stocks with significant potential for higher growth rates in sales, earnings, margins, and return on equity.

Value and growth investing are often presented as somewhat contrasting strategies of investing. But many investment experts tend to disagree and believe that the most important factor in investing is the intrinsic value that, inter alia, incorporates the growth rate of the company. However, our experience suggests that value-investing approach is more suitable for well-qualified investors. Generally, knowledgeable professionals are good at examining the company's fundamentals, which provide the definite clues as against the probability of future growth anticipated in growth investing.

Moreover, it is essential to go beyond these strategies and examine other crucial subjective factors such as management credibility, industry potential, business cycles, past track records and future forecasts. A prudent investment approach calls for a suitable blend of growth and value stocks in your portfolio so that you have the requisite flexibility to deal with the vagaries of the volatile world of equities on the way to make fortunes in the long haul.

Further, investing can be based on bottom-up or top-down approach. What we have discussed above is primarily a bottom up approach wherein investors focus on microeconomics of the particular stocks. Here starting point is the current market price of the sock, which is examined with reference to fundamentals of the company to decide whether it is undervalued or overvalued. Top down approach, on the other hand, has more to do with macroeconomic factors such as national growth rates, inflation, interest rates, currency rates and economic climate. Top down approach seeks to identify potential sectors or stocks based on the broad economic parameters.

Equity investing can be a simple or elaborate exercise, as you want it to be. A veteran investor can take advantage of the complex strategies by participating in derivatives (futures &

options), convertible securities, preference stocks, private equity, etc. Whether you are a new investor or an expert investor with time constraints, you can profit from indirect equity investing through mutual fund route, which we will examine after analyzing the major asset classes. You can make good use of the following standard table to determine how equity investment fit in your investment plan.

Equity Investment Evaluation Template

Criteria / Factors	Standard Observations	Your Perspective
A. Investment		
Risk	Medium to high	...
Income	Low to medium	
Capital appreciation	Medium to high	
Volatility	Medium to high	
Liquidity	Usually high	...
B. Personal		
Goals	Suits Long-Term wealth creation	
Knowledge	Very important	
Temperament	Crucial	
Time horizon	Preferably flexible	
Asset allocation	20-70% based on personal profile	....

After comprehending the above table, it would be easier for an individual to work out the right equity component in her or his portfolio. Here we outline the advantages and disadvantages of equity investments to facilitate you to take a considered call on equity.

Advantages

+ Offers an excellent opportunity with a proven track record of creating wealth
+ Enables you to take advantage of your knowledge to maximize your gains and minimize losses
+ Provides you an opportunity to take part in the growth of company and economy
+ Volatility provides a source of income to traders, investors and arbitrageurs
+ Fetched the best returns among all financial instruments in the last century
+ Wide variety to pick your picks compatible with your investment goals.

Disadvantages

- Can be quite risky for an uninitiated or overconfident investor
- Often timing the purchases or sales is not workable
- High volatility can undermine investors' confidence
- High probability of losing the capital due to leveraged trading or market swings
- Quick gains can overwhelm and tempt the naïve investor to derail his planned asset allocation
- Demands time, energy and resources to effectively participate.

Fixed Income Investments

It is a safe and dependable investment category, which offers the basic kind of secure and defined return products. These products are considered more conservative investments than stocks. People do not recognize fixed income investments as true wealth creating vehicles. Even then, this category attracts the lion's share of incremental savings owing to its low risk and high liquidity parameters. And the inflow is not just from people seeking regular income. Prudent investors also prefer to fall back on fixed return instruments to temporarily park their funds.

It takes time and prudence to evaluate the various investment avenues to pick out the one that makes the money work harder to generate the desired returns. Until that time, judicious future planning requires a reasonable portion of financial assets in liquid fixed return products. It helps to take advantage of opportune and alluring investment opportunities or to meet other contingency needs. Shrewd investors also use this category to deal with overvaluation in other asset classes or to gain from market volatility from time to time.

The fixed income investments reduce the risk as well as overall volatility of the portfolio. Conservative investors have a special liking for this category, as these investments generally do not pose any risk to their capital. Further, these instruments are normally simple to understand and do not require specialized domain knowledge. However, it should be ensured that yield is good enough to offset the inflation impact. Yield is the return that an investment brings in periodically, as interest from bonds and debt products, dividend from stocks and rent from real estate. While investing in debt products, we must remember that yield is important, as it is the primary objective and not the capital appreciation.

There are number of products to invest in this category such as Bonds, Treasury Bills, Certificate of Deposit and commercial Paper. Investment in bonds, etc. is very safe and can provide regular returns based on the coupon rate of bond. The issuer decides coupon rate and your bond yield will be equal to coupon rate if you have purchased bond at the original price. When you buy the bond at the prevailing market price, your bond yield will depend on your purchase price. If you buy bond at a premium, i.e., above its issue price, your bond yield will be less than the coupon rate. Similarly, if you buy bond at a discount, your yield will be more than the coupon rate as well as you will get the discount amount at the time of maturity. While the bond yields may fluctuate with changes in the bond prices, absolute return to the long-term investor remains the same.

Many investment experts prefer to keep preference shares and debentures under the fixed income category of the portfolio since return on these instruments is fixed and price volatility is not a major issue. Similarly, convertible bonds or debentures are also included in this category until the date of conversion. Here are a few pointers to help you to determine the percentage of fixed income securities in your portfolio.

Fixed Income Investment Evaluation Template

Criteria/ Factors	Standard Observations	Your Perspective
A. Investment		
Risk	Low	
Income	Low	
Capital Appreciation	Not Relevant (NA)	
Volatility	N.A./Low	
Liquidity	Usually High	
B. Personal		
Goals	Capital preservation & Contingency	
Knowledge	Not very relevant	
Temperament	Not very relevant	
Time horizon	Fixed/ Not relevant	
Asset allocation	10-60% depending on personal profile	

Advantages
+ The most reliable source of virtually assured returns
+ Simple and Clear-cut investment avenue
+ Experience and temperament are not very relevant
+ Enables flight to safety whenever other asset classes are overvalued
+ Provides a reasonable hedge against inflation
+ Market risk and market timing risk are nearly absent.

Disadvantages
− Risk of default in some cases
− Not suitable for real capital accretion
− Interest rate fluctuations or non-payment risk
− Opportunity loss in case of delay in payment

–   Probability of capital erosion when inflation surpasses interest.

Real Estate

A real (and really useful) asset that you can hold in your portfolio is real estate. Realty is a good risk diversifier as well as an excellent wealth creation tool. It can also provide regular income as rent or savings on rent. Further, it is less volatile as compared to other investments, and its low correlation with other asset classes makes it an ideal investment for a well-diversified portfolio.

Most people consider themselves quite knowledgeable in real estate assets, especially in their familiar settings. Surprisingly, they are right in their analysis eight times out of ten, which is an exceptionally good success rate by any investing yardstick. However, it is a different kind of asset class where supply is somewhat constrained and demand is bound to rise. Moreover, here it is comparatively easier to predict market forces of demand and supply if one can see through the irrational exuberance or unfair skepticism.

However, investing in real estate is not an easy task. It calls for a good knowledge, as the ticket size is usually very large as compared to other investments. So, investors must be wary of various risks, such as location risk, title risk, market risk, security concerns and property type risk, and carefully consider these before committing their capital. This is very important because real estate assets are normally long-term investments and involve a good amount of capital. However, one can overcome many of these off-putting factors by investing through real estate funds if the need for abode is not relevant.

In spite of everything, the most coveted asset class is real estate, greatly desired and highly preferred. Traditionally, investors consider real estate as the foremost investment in the form of a house ownership. The house not only provides security and comfort to the owner, but also results in savings on rent in addition to capital gains. The right real estate investment in your abode can change your life. This is why it makes for such a rewarding investment.

Most people prefer to keep it out of the purview of the investment planning process. The first home is a necessity for everyone. So, different circumstances of different people can justify any proportion of real estate component in their total assets in the form of a dwelling unit. However, when the value of house is more than 70% of total assets, it should be partly financed at reasonable interest rate. The idea is to deploy this part in other assets to avoid concentration of capital in one asset class and have a more diversified investment portfolio. Further, when you are buying a real estate to stay, even the price and risk-return ratio is to be seen in that context since the extra premium paid is most likely to even out in the long haul. These features prompt investment experts to recommend a differential treatment to this asset by keeping it out of asset allocation format. However, investments in a second home or vacation home or any other property should be reckoned as portfolio investments. These must be incorporated in asset allocation table when primary purpose of these investments is probable capital appreciation or rental income.

Further, investment in real estate can be done in many ways. For instance, investors can take exposure to real estate in their portfolio through land, residential properties, office spaces, farmhouses, shopping complex, ventures with major investment in real estate, industrial complex, real estate mutual funds, etc. However, preferences should be accorded to the geographical location which one understands well, and where one can easily organize the requisite upkeep of the property.

Historically, it has been seen that the right real estate investments give the best combination of safety and returns. There are many factors to justify investments in real estate, but predominantly it comes down to the dynamics of demand and supply. While the demand is increasing, the supply at macro level is limited leading to decent appreciation in the prime locations. Real estate component is a must for investors' portfolio for efficient and gainful asset allocation. Investment experts agree that real estate is an excellent diversifier within a portfolio. It is a good choice for long-term, risk averse and financially disinclined investors who are seeking higher returns as well as a hedge against inflation to protect their capital. Many people, who are wary of the intricacies and uncertainties of financial investments, opt for real estate as their primary investment avenue. You can examine this investment vehicle from your perspective with the help of this table.

Real Estate Investment Evaluation Template

Criteria / Factors	Standard Observations	Your Perspective
A. Investment		
Risk	Low to medium	
Income	Low	
Capital appreciation	Medium to high	
Volatility	Low to medium	
Liquidity	Medium	
B. Personal		
Goals	Suits long-term wealth creation	
Knowledge	Important	
Temperament	Not very relevant	
Time horizon	Medium to long term	
Asset allocation	10-50% depending on personal profile	

Further, the following advantages and disadvantages of real estate investments attempt to put this investment avenue in true perspective.

Advantages

+   A potential source of rental income or savings in rent
+   Potential for multiplying returns with financial leverage (using low-interest, borrowed funds)
+   Effective hedge against inflation as the supply is virtually limited
+   Probable tax benefits

+   Great potential for capital appreciation
+   Own home provides comfort, security and stability.

Disadvantages
−   Risk of concentration of property in portfolio
−   Restricted market and liquidity concerns
−   Probability of value erosion
−   Difficult to assess real value
−   Complex documentation
−   Requires upkeep as well as maintenance expenses, municipal taxes, etc.
−   Susceptible to geographical and economic problems.

Precious Metals

Jewelry, the oldest form of body ornament, is usually made of different precious metals like gold, silver and platinum, and sometimes also contains precious stones like diamonds, pearls and gemstones. Since ancient times, people buy precious metals in the form of jewelry for its esteem value as well as for its proven ability to preserve value over time. But primary consideration used to be the ornamental value and not the investment worth.

After experiencing a significant increase in the prices of these metals in the recent years, nowadays investors are rediscovering the allure of this evergreen investment avenue. They are eager to diversify a part of their investments in these all weather products in the pursuit of wealth creation in addition to wealth preservation. Many others are looking at gold and silver to ring fence their capital.

The high levels of liquidity that chased all assets, including precious metals, have also influenced the historical demand-supply balance of these assets. Historically this balance gets disturbed in turbulent times leading to a surge in the prices of precious metals, just when other volatile investments suffer free fall. Accordingly, these assets are considered as defensive assets more suitable for conservative investors. However, the recent upswings in prices as a result of demand outstripping supply in normal times have repositioned these assets from their low risk-low return and defensive status to a much sought after investment option. That is why many defensive investments like gold and silver are again finding favor with all types of investors in this ever-changing economic world.

Investment in precious metals like gold, silver and platinum is a time tested investment strategy to provide an effective hedge against inflation as well as a real security in the tumultuous times. They also provide an excellent protection against currency, political, economic and default risks. Moreover, these real assets in the form of gold, silver, etc. are truly regarded as a global currency and as such are the most liquid and comforting assets. So, having precious metals in your portfolio is the right way to beat the vagaries of the investment world to ensure absolute liquidity as well as capital preservation. Investment in precious metals can be done in many ways such as physical, depository or certificate form, and exchange traded funds. Depositories usually charge handling expenses in the range of 0.5% to 1% of the investment value for storage, insurance, etc. Gold and silver exchange traded funds (ETF) are increasingly becoming popular as they offer the most economical and convenient route to invest in this category. ETFs are like units that are traded on the exchanges just like ordinary equity shares.

Flow Chart Showing Working of Gold ETFs

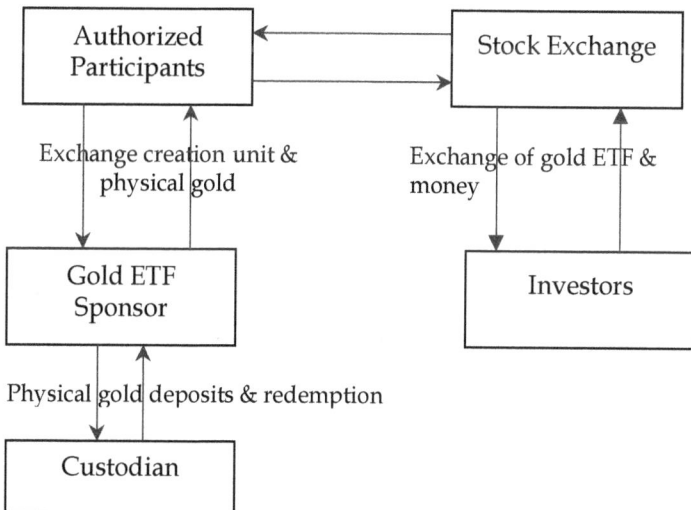

Here below we examine the standard investment criteria along with some pros and cons to help you to devise a suitable strategy to incorporate a bit of precious metals in your portfolio.

Precious Metals Investment Evaluation Template

Criteria / Factors	Standard Observations	Your Perspective
A. Investment		
Risk	Low to medium	
Income	Not applicable	
Capital appreciation	Medium	...
Volatility	Medium	
Liquidity	High	
B. Personal		
Goals	Suits wealth preservation	...
Knowledge	Not very important	
Temperament	Not very relevant	.....
Time horizon	Not relevant	
Asset allocation	0-20%	11.5%

Advantages
+ Precious metals offer high liquidity and low volatility
+ A low correlation between precious metals and other asset classes makes precious metals a good risk diversifier
+ Physical possession offers privacy, and sense of tangible assets, which can be easily transported
+ Demand is growing whereas supply is restricted
+ Immune to political or economic upheavals
+ Expert knowledge is not very important.

Disadvantages
- Value appreciation based on unpredictable market forces
- Not a source of income, conversely require upkeep expenses
- Keeping in jewelry form leads to value erosion
- Requires maintenance and safety measures
- Knowledge plays a little role in maximizing profit potential.

Artworks

Earlier art assets were considered an exclusive domain of the rich and famous. The elite class used to buy artworks primarily for its esteem value. In the last decade, most volatile investment vehicles such as equity, precious metals, commodities and real estate have outperformed their historical average returns. But amazingly, returns from art investments have outperformed all these categories. This is primarily due to the emergence of artwork as investment worthy asset class on the radar of many high net worth investors resulting in ever more demand for the scarce artwork of good quality. In the last two decades, art assets have generated phenomenal capital appreciation, which surpasses all other asset classes including major equity indices. Returns on art assets have outperformed nearly all equity indices over the last five decades. The dynamics of international art markets are such that always there has been an uptrend in prices barring occasional insignificant dips. This is because artwork is a niche market wherein many connoisseurs are chasing a limited supply of quality artworks. Experts expect this trend to continue in the predictable future as indicated by robust demand of good art assets.

Art is a very attractive investment option for real connoisseurs of artwork given that it provides them a real opportunity of capital appreciation while enjoying their passion. Such investors are in a better position to understand and appreciate the true worth of art assets. Nowadays art savvy people are increasingly donning the role of investors. They are more than willing to bear the upkeep expenses and low liquidity in their pursuit of wealth creation. All investors, who are willing to appreciate both artistic and financial aspects of art assets, can surely gain from this appealing asset class. However, they should not expect historical returns in future. The extraordinary returns of the past were because of two reasons. The first is about the demand-supply mismatch, which was further accentuated by the second reason, i.e., too much liquidity from the artificially low interest rates. However, like all other investments, artwork is also exposed to a few inherent risks, for instance it entails special upkeep, provides no income and is usually low on liquidity.

As art investments are yielding greater returns, more and more common investors aspire to include this in their portfolio. The first and foremost decision for an amateur investor is to select the right category of artwork such as paintings, sculpture, found objects, photography, collectibles and assemblages. New age artworks like offbeat sculptures and assemblages, which are a combination of different artworks including sculpture, paintings, etc. are particularly attracting investors. Many experts prefer to consider collectibles like coins, memorabilia and stamps in this category because of many similarities of market dynamics. Alternative mediums with fresh concepts and other novel kind of artworks are expected to hit the market in future to cope with the inadequate supply of artwork, and add further fuel to the art boom. The key to art investing lies in picking up that category where you sense the demand is growing and likely to remain upbeat in the predictable future. Further, you need to do your groundwork well in examining the artwork as well as assess your ability to preserve it in the right condition. In this asset class, it is vital that you understand well your chosen artwork because the quality of artwork plays a major role in the investment's risk-return ratio. For an inexpert investor, getting it right is as important as getting into the right art category.

The reputation of the artist is also a very important consideration. However, investors have to be watchful about the proliferation of fakes of the reputed artists and must be sure of the provenance before committing their money. Then again, if you are a sharp-eyed investor and can perceive where the art world is heading, you can pick the work of a lesser-known artist at a bargain price with good prospects of reaping great returns. It goes without saying that when you cannot work out the real worth of your chosen art, you must seek specialized guidance to pick the right artwork as well as to determine the trends in the art market.

Here are some advantages and disadvantages along with the standard criterion table to enable you to judge whether art assets can find a place on your walls as well as in your portfolio.

Artwork Investment Evaluation Template

Criteria / Factors	Standard Observations	Your Perspective
A. Investment		
Risk	Medium	
Income	Not applicable	
Capital appreciation	High	...
Volatility	Low to medium	
Liquidity	Low	..?
B. Personal		
Goals	Suits wealth creation	
Knowledge	Crucial	...
Temperament	Not very relevant	
Time horizon	Medium to long term	
Asset allocation	0-15%	10.5%

Advantages
+ Tangible and real assets provide sense of possession
+ Good returns offer huge potential for wealth creation
+ Have the benefit of decorative and esteem value
+ Demand is incessantly growing at a faster pace than supply of quality artwork
+ More and more investors perceive it as the most appreciating investment, resulting in increased demand
+ Develops creative and discerning disposition.

Disadvantages
- Not a source of income, on the contrary require expenses for preservation
- Lacks standardization, transparency and liquidity
- Very risky for an uninitiated investor
- Maintenance and upkeep require time, energy and money
- Difficult to calculate intrinsic value
- Risk of obsolescence in some categories.

Commodities

Commodities are standard things of value that are produced in large quantities by many different producers. Commodities include all unbranded and normally traded goods of standardized quality. Soft commodities are goods that are grown, while hard commodities are extracted through mining. Unlike other asset classes, commodities are ubiquitous.

We all deal with commodities such as fuels, agriculture products, base metals and energy in our everyday life. Yet, most of us are reluctant to take the plunge as investors in this unique asset class. Even though many of us have deeper understanding of the market forces affecting demand and supply of a few commodities because of our professional association or otherwise, we do not seriously consider capitalizing on this knowledge. This knowledge can open a very exciting investment alternative, which has the potential to offer excellent returns to investors who are good at correctly forecasting the future trends in select commodities.

Financial aspects of commodities are quite similar to precious metals barring the fact that commodities are essentially consumption driven items whereas the precious metals are primarily used for decorative or hoarding purposes. This implies that growth in the demand of commodities is almost a certainty in view of the increasing population and ever-increasing consumption trends due to continually improving lifestyles. This likely demand and supply mismatch points to the robust demand for essential commodities in the foreseeable future. Further, genuine investments in commodities represent only a small percentage of overall investments. This under ownership of commodities as investments and the strong probability of demand outstripping supply in many of the commodities augers well for this investment avenue. However, before rushing headlong into commodities, investors should keep in mind that often these obvious future trends are not correctly reflected in the market prices. Often irrational exuberance and market momentum can take the prices to artificially high levels. In the long-term, market price of any commodity will indicate the true value. But in the short-term, there are many other factors influencing the price and thus making it volatile. Except for this volatility, commodities are likely to give reasonably good capital appreciation over longer periods. Prudent investors take into account the interplay of price determining factors as well as other variables like global factors, weather, consumption trends, social factors, government policies, and the rest before committing their funds. And, more importantly, they do not buy or sell any product, which they do not understand well.

Investment in commodities is a good portfolio diversifier as well as an excellent hedge against the perils of inflation. It is a good alternative for investors who are circumspect about the obscure and volatile financial investments but are seeking higher returns. Investment in commodities could be either delivery based or through derivatives, i.e., futures and options market. Most participants in commodities take positions through futures contract wherein they are just required to deposit a small margin until the settlement date when they can close out the position by selling or buying that contract. However, many equity savvy investors prefer to take part in commodity investments indirectly through equity route by investing in the shares of commodity companies.

Commodity investment per se is not as popular as other portfolio investments. Lately, it is catching the attention of well-informed investors, and future growth looks to be quite promising. However, trading volumes of global commodity trade is huge as compared to trading volumes of any other asset class. At present, usually the traders, hedgers, consumers and manufacturers make good use of commodity exchanges and provide the requisite liquidity to the market. Here are a few indicators to facilitate you to make up your mind whether commodity investments go well with your portfolio.

Commodities Investment Evaluation Template

Criteria/Factors	Standard Observations	Your Perspective
A. Investment		
Risk	Medium	
Income	Not applicable	
Capital appreciation	Medium to high	
Volatility	Medium	
Liquidity	Reasonable	
B. Personal		
Goals	Suits wealth creation	
Knowledge	Very Important	
Temperament	Important	
Time horizon	Variable	
Asset allocation	0-25%	

Advantages

+ Investment in real and essential assets
+ Commodities are under-owned as investments
+ Best antidote to the risk of higher inflation
+ Supply is constrained while demand is rising
+ Enables informed investors to profit from their good judgment.

Disadvantages

− Forecasting global market forces is inherently a tricky task
− Sometimes certain commodities can be highly volatile for longer periods
− Leveraged investments in derivative contracts can result in losing the entire capital

- Commodity cycles may or may not follow earlier trends
- Generally, making money through trading is overwhelming even for the skilled traders.

The purpose of above discussion is to familiarize you with the broad features of common asset classes so as to enable you to take informed decisions while finalizing your asset allocation. One positive aspect of so many investment options is that you can participate in any asset class even if you are not well equipped to manage that particular investment category. For instance, if you are not well versed with equity investments but keen to participate in this lucrative avenue, you can directly invest in equity through exchange-traded funds, index units or other derivative options. Further, if you do not have time or expertise to deal with your preferred investment vehicles, where knowledge plays a crucial role, but have intense desire to invest, you may do so indirectly through mutual funds. We will take up these indirect investment avenues after discussing how investors should select their optimal portfolios.

3.4 Building Portfolio: What to Pick and What to Skip

When it comes to choosing investments, investors have innumerable choices. While such a large variety of options allows investors to customize their investment portfolio to suit their personal needs and objectives, it makes the investment selection process somewhat overwhelming for many. Having such a large range is more of a hindrance than a benefit for many investors, especially when there is not any standard yardstick or formula to help investors choose a compatible asset mix and pick specific investments in each asset class. What's more, there is no such thing as the perfect portfolio, much like there is no such thing as the perfect job or perfect spouse. And choosing investments for the portfolio combines elements of both science and art.

Investors have to decide themselves what to pick and what to skip to finalize their investment portfolio. 'What to pick and what to skip' may not work in the case of your job or spouse, but here it is workable since you are the boss. But with authority comes accountability.

For a self-aware, prudent investor, picking the right investments may not be very difficult. You can also choose the winning investments easily if you know your financial goals, understand yourself as an investor and ready to explore the investment opportunities.

While discussing investing basics, we have seen that the first step to successful investing is appreciating your investment objectives. You should be clear about your important financial goals, time frame to reach these goals and how much money you need. Once you know why you are investing, when you will need the money, and how much risk you can endure, you can easily decide what to pick and what to skip. Here is a simple financial goals format depicting timelines and the money required to reach your goals and also a brief narrative on how your goals prompt you to explore appropriate investments.

Financial Goals Worksheet

Goals	Time Frame/ Priority	Amount Required
Create a Contingency Fund	ASAP/ High	50000
To Buy a House	9Years/ High	...
Save for Child's education	7 Years/ High	...
World Tour/Vacation	Flexible/Low	...
Buy a new Car	2 Years/ Medium	...
Savings for Retirement	25 years/ High	...
Build Wealth	25 years/ Medium	....

In the case of short-term goals, i.e., less than two years (e.g., creating a contingency fund, vacation, buying a new car), you need to choose safe investments, which are easy to convert to cash. You can seek secure returns, but your prime consideration should be liquidity. So for this category, you need low risk, assured/fixed return kind of investments.

In the case of medium-term goals, i.e., between two and seven years (e.g., child's education), you have time to seek good returns from dependable investments like equity, debt and precious metals. Here you can seek growth with moderate risk-return balance.

In the case of long-term goals, i.e., more than seven years away (e.g., savings for retirement, to buy a house and build wealth), you have time on your side, and you can afford to be a bit aggressive to seek high growth. You have many years before you will need the cash. So, even if you suffer losses, you have time to cover up. But remember, this money is important for securing your future. Here you can shrewdly seek aggressive growth and invest a part of your portfolio in high-risk, high-return securities.

After empathizing with your cherished financial goals, the next step is to understand yourself as an investor. When you really understand yourself better as an investor, it will be easier to make investment choices that are right for you. Harvard professor Richard Geist, who has done pioneering research on investor psychology, points out that, first, investors need to learn about and understand their investment psychology. When investors become aware of their own unique psychology, they can adapt it to market conditions.

Psychological factors play an influential role in investing success. It is important to clarify the underlying psychological thought process relating to your financial habits before you choose your investments. In the words of legendary investor Warren Buffett, "To invest successfully over a lifetime does not require a stratospheric IQ, unusual business insight, or inside information. What's needed is a sound intellectual framework for decisions and the ability to keep emotions from corroding the framework." So, you need to watch your emotions closely or they can derail your investing plan. It is better to behave like a robot while managing your investments.

Besides, many investors tend to give due attention to their purchases, including small everyday purchases like groceries, fruits or vegetables. But when it comes to analyzing their major investments, they starkly brush aside the requisite due diligence process. And then there are some risk-averse investors, who are not comfortable with market volatility, but they do not appreciate their risk tolerance level before investing. So, they get panicky when their investments swing on the downside, and irrationally liquidate investments to book losses. Then again, some people impulsively follow media hype or tips from friends, thereby making their investments vulnerable to various risks.

A well-researched investment decision could be a bit time consuming, but it assures the quality of our investments and assures the preferred risk-return ratio. We must remember that these are essentially long-term decisions, which may not have any significant bearing on our everyday life but can have sweeping implications for future. So, it is in our interest to pay the due attention and devote requisite time to examine our investments with reference to our risk-return quotient.

We have already discussed in the previous chapters the role of investor temperament, risk tolerance levels and returns expectations in the game of investing. We have also seen that investors' knowledge and life stages have some significant impact on their risk-return quotient. Now we take up the risk-return quotient in the context of various asset classes. We are illustrating here below a tentative placement of all the asset classes discussed in the previous chapter in the all-important risk-return matrix. But this should not be considered as a hard and fast rule. It is just a simplistic generalization, as nobody has yet found the perfect formula to determine the exact risk-return placement of various asset classes.

Risk-Return Placement of Various Asset Classes

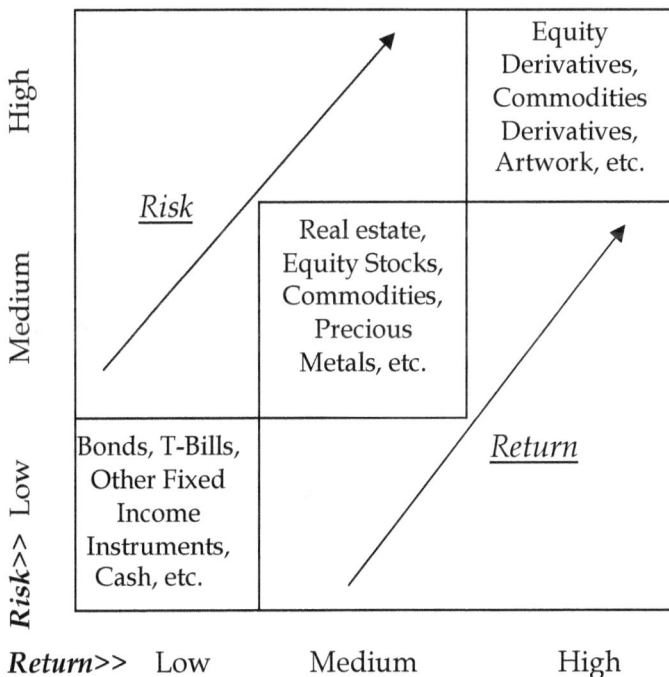

In fact, the exact risk-return placement is influenced by the specific investment option in conjunction with the investor's personal profile. We cannot have a very simple and standard answer to such an intricate question. In fact, this zillion-dollar question is the ultimate key to wealth creation. Further, dynamic nature of markets demands some hard work and prudence to assess the suitability of various asset classes at a particular time and determine their suitability for a particular investor at that time. That is why many times market levels or trends call for planned procrastination rather than rushing headlong in this game of investing.

The above matrix highlights the broad pointers to facilitate initial exploratory exercise to determine likely ingredients of your investment portfolio. These pointers do not take into account the third dimension of time, which can significantly alter risk return equilibrium through different time horizons. For example, risk in equities normally decreases with time and as such, one can expect higher returns with medium risk in equities over a long haul. Further, the above placements do not give enough emphasis to the knowledge and behavioral aspects, which play a crucial role in many asset classes. With the positive interplay of these aspects, risk to rewards ratio tends to twist towards rewards. Investors need to double-check which of these asset classes are suitable for them before finalizing their asset allocation. However, it should not be a one-off exercise in the dynamic world of investments.

Concentrating investments concentrates risk. Diversifying investments dilutes risk. Investing in various asset classes reduces your exposure to economic, asset class and market risks and maximizes your potential returns for that amount of risk. And selecting different investments within each asset class further diversifies your portfolio and reduces risk while seeking optimal returns.

Many experts prefer to select asset classes and specific investments in each asset class on the basis of investor's financial goals. We broadly agree with this approach, but prefer that first, asset allocation should be determined with reference to investor's profile, capital available and market situation. At this stage, we should be indifferent to the investor's specific financial goals, which can be linked to the settled asset allocation in the next step. However, risk-return attitude and broad timelines for the most important goals always remain at the back of investors' mind. So, with a view to reap maximum benefits of this proven strategy, we intend to just focus on the asset mix at this stage. We feel considering financial goals before deciding the asset mix runs the risk of diverting attention, and thus diluting the potential benefits of the asset allocation strategy. Moreover, financial goals are dynamic and somewhat fungible in nature, and in any case, we are going to link these with the asset mix in the next step.

However, one can skip this step if only incremental savings are to be invested to realize the financial goals. But one should make an action plan describing how the financial goals will be realized through monthly savings. The following worksheet is intended to help investors clarify their savings potential as well as give them clarity, direction and pathway to achieve their goals.

Financial Goals and Savings Plan

Goals	Target Date	Amount	Monthly Saving	Action Plan
(specific)	(preferred)	(specific)	(realistic)	(practical)
Buy a new car	1 year	...	...	..., ..., ...

Where significant capital is involved, determining first the asset allocation in isolation to financial goals is a desirable strategy since it helps to preserve and grow total capital. Here, our first objective is to maximize overall returns and minimize overall risk of the portfolio.

The asset allocation strategy seeks to distribute your money across various asset classes so that the poor performance of any asset class does not jeopardize your financial vision. While discussing the basics of successful investing, we have seen that the asset allocation is the most important investment decision that involves determining what percentage of a portfolio should be allocated to each asset class. And this diversification across asset classes gives you a lot of flexibility to manage market uncertainties to your advantage in the long haul. The asset allocation decision is a very personal one. Your best-fit asset allocation is unique to you, and it changes at different times in your life depending on your life stages and other personal factors.

You are aware of the basic factors affecting investing success. You also know how they can make your money work harder for you. Once you understand these, determining your optimum asset mix will be very easy for you. To allocate your capital efficiently, you can use the following format to record your existing as well as intended asset mix in percentage and/or absolute numbers.

Asset Allocation Worksheet

(Percentage)

Asset Class	Present	Planned
Equity Investments		
Fixed Return Investments		
Real Estate		
Precious Metals		
Art Assets		
Commodities		
Cash/ Cash Equivalent		

Since markets are dynamic and ever changing, you need to rebalance your portfolio in order to keep it in line with your investment objectives. There are two common approaches to portfolio rebalancing, viz., strategic approach and tactical approach. In strategic approach, you periodically rebalance your assets to your original target asset mix. In tactical approach, you rebalance your asset mix based on market opportunities and economic changes, using acceptable ranges for each asset class.

Investment planning is a lifelong learning process. You can always improve your asset allocation. You can always revisit it and change it for the better. But frequent or unnecessary changes are not desirable, as they make the process somewhat cumbersome and unstable. While periodical reviews and remedial measures are necessary, one should resist the temptation to make changes just for the sake of change.

Moreover, here you are not supposed to seek 100% arithmetical accuracy. Plus or minus 5% should be ignored to keep the process simple. In investment planning, there are many factors which cannot be accurately forecasted. Investments, where you can forecast your returns with conviction, present a typical challenge to preserve the purchasing power of your money, particularly in the long run. So, here you can take some liberty with the accuracy in order to keep your investing plan simple. However, you should not compromise on the basic factors that influence investing success.

After broadly deciding your asset mix, you have to pick individual investments for each asset class. You should select winning investments for your portfolio depending on the amount of capital available to invest and your financial goals. It is here where your knowledge, shrewdness and expertise will play its role to pick rewarding investments. To win the investing game, remember, your picks should be in harmony with your asset allocation, risk/reward analysis and your financial goals.

Now you should tentatively link your financial goals with your investments. This will give you confidence that allocated investments will yield targeted amount by the targeted time. With a view to simplify your exercise and put your goals and investments in perspective, the following worksheet illustrates how you can classify your goals based on time horizons and then apportion your asset mix for each goal. After that, you can select specific investments within each asset class considering your priorities. Here, you are supposed to create your own allocation model by entering percentages (and amounts if you want) against each asset class and specific investments in the second and third columns respectively. Percentages must be whole numbers and total must equal 100.

Investment Allocation Model

Goals	Asset Class Description	%	Investments Description	%
Short Term: Contingency fund	...	..	...+ ...	
Vacation	...	.	...+...+	
Buy a new car	...	.	...+...+...+	
Medium Term: Child's education				
Long Term: Saving for retirement Buy a house Build wealth				
Total		100%		100%

There is no single investment allocation model that is right for everyone. And there is no standard way to create it. Only you can positively contribute to your personal goals. So, whatever investments you choose, the key is to understand how they work and how they will help you to achieve your particular financial goal. And before you buy any investment, you should be clear about the following questions.

» Do I understand how this investment works?
» Am I seeking safety, income, or growth from this investment?
» How much can I hope to make from this investment?
» Do I have good information about this specific investment?
» Can I forecast how it will perform in future?
» Do I understand the risk-reward quotient of this investment?
» What is my expected time horizon for this investment?
» Do I have alternative if it does not perform as expected?

Investors often choose their initial investments on the basis of an objective criterion, but once they own the investments, they run the risk of becoming possessive and emotional about their investments. Investors should never fall in love with an investment. They should never get emotionally involved to their investments and adamantly cling on to them. Investors should keep in mind that winning and losing are both involved in the game of investing, and they should be prepared to take occasional losses in stride and learn from them. The investments are a means to achieve goals and not goals by themselves. Further, to accentuate the golden rules, here we reiterate the main points that help investing in general.

✓ Investigate the investment prior to investing.
✓ Control emotions and cultivate the right temperament.
✓ Avoid leveraged investing, i.e. investing with borrowed money.
✓ Invest 100 minus your age in the high-risk, high-return investments, i.e. the percentage of volatile investments should be a decreasing function of your age.
✓ Beware of unscrupulous intermediaries.
✓ Be contrarian. Use irrational behavior of the markets to your advantage. Look for bargains during panic time and book partial profits in times of euphoria.
✓ Be wary of tips. During bullish phase, one thing that rises as fast as returns is advice, not good advice.
✓ Beware of herd mentality. Remember self-regulation is the key to successful investing.

- ✓ Do not buy and forget. Never sleep over your investments, periodically review them.
- ✓ Do not be possessive. Book a loss if your view of the investment changes.
- ✓ If price of your investment falls, you can buy more to average your acquisition cost provided you continue to have conviction in the fundamentals of your investment.
- ✓ Avoid momentum trading, especially when you do not have the requisite wherewithal and time to closely monitor it.
- ✓ Avoid irrational exuberance and 'get-rich-quick' plans.
- ✓ Ignore short-term price fluctuations for long-term assets and stay the course because the power of compounding is amazing.
- ✓ Continue only with such investments that you can understand and monitor. While managing your personal portfolio, remember that the key word is 'personal' since you are not accountable to anyone but yourself.
- ✓ Invest with your head, not with your heart.

Some investors get overwhelmed while evaluating some asset classes, as they do not have the time and expertise to understand the nuances of various asset classes. They suppose that it is not their calling. In spite of that they can participate in any asset class through mutual funds wherein investment professionals invest for them into their desired asset classes. We will discuss this indirect investing route in the next chapter.

It takes a little dose of wisdom along with a clear-cut and structured process to examine the various investable assets to make your money work harder for you. Historically, it has been seen that well-informed investors make money and ill-informed people lose money. In spite of that occasionally frivolous investors and speculators do make good money while dancing with the bulls or shooting with the bears in the volatile world of investments. But sincere investors should bear in mind that speculators may outshine you even without any drudgery in the short term but invariably well-informed investors thrive in the ultimate analysis of lifetime investing.

Part 4

The Outsourcing of Money Making

4.1 Understanding Mutual Funds

We are now familiar with many investable asset classes, which are more than sufficient to accomplish any conceivable investment objective. These investment avenues were discussed in the chapter "The Investing Universe: Understanding Asset Classes" presupposing direct investment approach wherein investors invest on their own. However, most of the better investment avenues call for a significant domain knowledge as well as expertise to analyze the specific investments, which many individual investors may not possess. Further, direct investment approach often demands constant monitoring of portfolio to facilitate opportune decision-making. But, many of us may not have the time or requisite wherewithal to successfully monitor our investments.

In view of these prerequisites to successful investing, many investors opt for external expertise to manage their investments in an optimal manner. Mutual funds offer investors a simple, efficient and less time-consuming method of investing wherein they delegate investment decisions to the mutual funds' managers. Mutual funds are an indirect means of investing in securities. In this chapter, we will discuss how to make money with mutual funds.

A mutual fund is a professionally managed trust that pools investors' money to buy certain assets such as equity, bonds and commodities. Investing through mutual funds is a passive investment method wherein several people with common investment objectives pool their money and arrange for the requisite expertise and resources to manage their investments efficiently. A mutual fund is such a financial intermediary that collects funds from investors and invests in appropriate assets as mandated by the investors. It offers an alternative investment avenue to investors who are interested in any particular investment option or a mix of investment options but do not possess the proficiency and/or time to invest on their own. Such an arrangement invariably offers several specialized advantages over direct investing, particularly in complex but rewarding investments. The next diagram broadly describes the working of a mutual fund.

Working of a Mutual Fund - Flow Chart

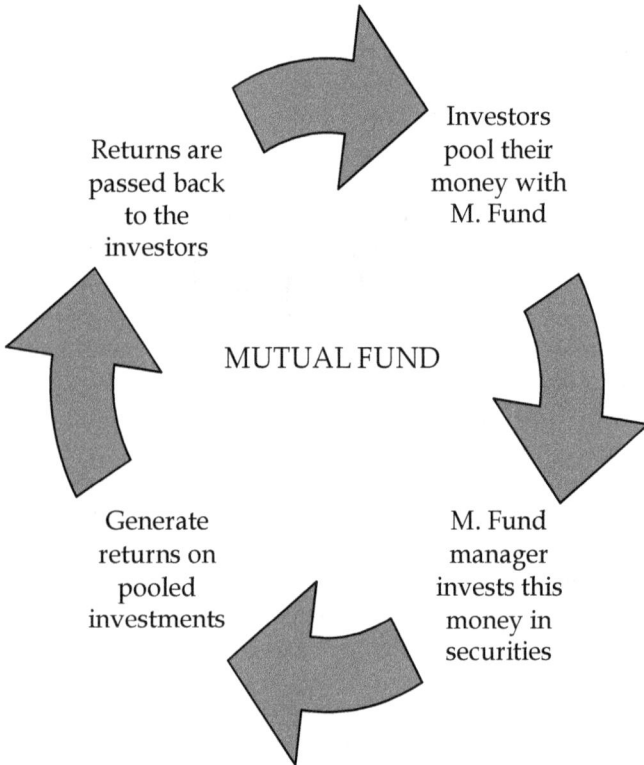

Returns are passed back to the investors

Investors pool their money with M. Fund

MUTUAL FUND

Generate returns on pooled investments

M. Fund manager invests this money in securities

A mutual fund is usually an independent entity, which charges a fee, mostly in terms of percentage of assets under management, for its services. Generally, investors can buy or sell a mutual fund's shares or units at its net assets value (NAV), which is simply the net worth of the fund's portfolio divided by the number of outstanding shares. NAV is usually computed daily on the basis of closing prices of all the investments of the fund. So, the NAV of a mutual fund essentially depends on the market value of its underlying investments. Most funds adopt a benchmark, which is typically an index selected by the fund company to serve as a yardstick to measure its performance. The benchmark also gives a rough and ready idea of type of investments fund manager will make.

This investment method allows uninitiated investors to passively participate in the investment avenues that they like, but do not understand. Inexperienced investors should preferably invest through the mutual fund route to cash in on the investment opportunities safely through a professional investment manager who is invariably well versed with the intricacies of related assets and is aptly equipped to meet the stated investment objectives. Investors are simply required to select the mutual fund, which is compatible with their personal profiles and investment goals. The mutual fund route is the best way to go for retail investors who do not know how to cherry pick the investments.

Mutual fund investors can depend on the fund manager who is predictably an expert in the relevant asset category and competent enough to pick and manage investments considering all the pertinent factors. The fund manager has to work as per the mandate of the fund. There are many entities involved in the working of a mutual fund and the fund manager works under a defined organizational setup.

It is always better to have a look at all the aspects before taking any investment advice at face value. So, any prudent investor would certainly like to consider the advantages and disadvantages of investing via mutual funds.

Advantages

Professional management: Specialist fund managers can exploit their expertise to maximize gains. Mutual fund staff can devote exclusive time to search for the better opportunities and research investments appropriately before committing.

Diversification: Mutual funds usually have greater buying power to own a variety of investments to construct a well-diversified portfolio, which an individual investor cannot match. Since a mutual fund holds well-diversified investment portfolio, its success is not contingent on the performance of a few investments.

Transaction costs: Mutual funds enjoy economy of scale and as such benefit from much greater buying power than an individual investor does. The expenses associated with buying and selling investments are spread among all the mutual fund shareholders.

Minimum investment: Mutual funds offer lowest per unit investment in most of the asset classes. The requirement of minimum investment is usually very small in most mutual funds. In many investment avenues such as real estate, artwork and the like, many small investors cannot invest directly owing to a large per unit investment. Mutual funds provide a way in to such small investors by offering very small lot sizes to invest.

Risk minimization: Normally investing through mutual funds entails less risk due to the optimum interplay of several factors essential for risk minimization. Here, professionals take investment decisions within a clear-cut and structured process that obviates the chances of rash and impulsive decisions. So, the overall risk in direct investing is much more than the mutual fund investments.

Constant monitoring: Dedicated fund managers can keep constant tabs on the investments in the portfolio with an eye to fine-tune the portfolio as and when required. Well-timed decisions can facilitate to cash in on the ups and downs of the market by successfully riding the surges in the markets and adapting a defensive approach when the markets correct.

Liquidity and Convenience: The majority of mutual funds are open-ended funds that provide ample liquidity at the prevailing market prices. In order to liquidate a part of portfolio, investors need not take the trouble to research and select the specific investments to sell. Mutual funds have a clear upper hand in terms of liquidity and convenience in comparison to most other direct investments.

Temperament: Several financial experts, including legendary investor Warren Buffet consider temperament as the single most important factor for success or failure in the world of investments.

Investing through mutual funds minimizes the risks owing to the human temperament, and makes a case to derive some benefits from the positive temperament of the fund managers.

Systems: Mutual funds follow carefully planned systems to manage investments on a day-to-day basis leading to improved performance of the portfolio. Their structured systems enable them to switch the portfolio swiftly for the strongest possible performance.

Variety and Flexibility: Mutual funds offer all types of investment instruments to meet the needs of every kind of investor. No other investment avenue can match the variety, affordability and flexibility offered by the mutual funds. This is particularly true in respect of financial instruments, which offer unmatched variety as well as flexibility to enter, switch or relinquish the fund. With mutual funds, investors can luxuriate in buying or selling investments without much caring for diversification, asset allocation, search and research of investments.

Disadvantages

Management fees: Nearly all mutual funds charge management fees and/or high commissions to recoup their administrative and marketing expenses. Many mutual fund expenses are fixed costs, such as the salaries of the staff, utilities expenses, marketing and administration overheads, over which neither the management nor the investors have any control. Investors have to pay these expenses irrespective of the fund's performance. In other words, management fees are payable even in the case of mismanagement, i.e., when the fund underperforms its benchmark.

Investment risk: No investment can be insulated from the risks, and mutual funds are not the exception. Mutual funds are not immune to the various investment risks. Funds also carry all the risks related with the kind of investments that they make. For example, a commodities fund is likely to perform poorly when commodity prices are falling.

No power over assets: Investors do not enjoy direct ownership of the assets of the mutual fund. So, they usually find it difficult to relate to the fund's investments because sense of belonging in respect of assets controlled by the fund may be lacking. Generally, mutual funds do not provide the advantages of a custom-made portfolio to individual investors. Investors may find it difficult to identify with the assets of the fund and have to endure the feeling of a proxy owner.

Inadequate returns: Many actively managed funds fail to outperform their applicable benchmark indices. On many occasions even passively managed funds like index funds do not yield as much as the corresponding index due to high tracking errors. Even the funds with excellent past records cannot guarantee the repeat of performance in future. In fact, rarely any fund can consistently provide above average returns in the long haul.

No choice: Investors do not enjoy freedom of choice. They cannot decide what to buy and what to sell. They do not relish the sense of command to influence the decision making as they are neither involved in the process of picking the assets nor they can select the assets to be liquidated. Usually, they are not allowed to prescribe or proscribe any specific investment relating to the fund's portfolio.

Unfair practices: Many critics routinely draw attention to the widely prevalent unfair practices wherein many fund managers accept direct and indirect benefits including extravagant gifts in exchange for some favors conceded to trading associates and other businesses whereby presumably investor's interests are sacrificed to some extent. Secondly, fund managers often focus on attracting new customers to maximize their commissions and to increase the fund size. These practices may be beneficial for the fund and its staff, but may perhaps hurt the interests of its existing investors.

No discretion on income sharing: Income or dividend distribution among the real owners of the mutual fund is invariably at the discretion of the fund management within the parameters initially stated in the fund's prospectus. In the same way, investors are customarily not permitted to determine the amount or the timing of the distributions.

Considering the importance of having the right funds in the portfolio, it is important to explore the different types of mutual funds. In the next chapter, we will discuss the various mutual fund options available to retail investors.

4.2 Types of Mutual Funds

We have seen that mutual funds offer a convenient and disciplined way of investing that is devoid of personal bias and preconceived notions. Yet, it is not a walk in the park. One has to try hard to select the appropriate fund bearing in mind her or his profile as well as fund's past performance and likely future outlook. The numerous mutual funds ranging from equity, debt, real estate, commodities, precious metals, etc. to various mélange of some of these make this task even more challenging. With complex and volatile markets, the role of choosing the right fund has become crucial not only to build wealth, but also to preserve capital in terms of true purchasing power in these inflationary times.

Investors should have basic knowledge of various types of funds before devising a suitable investment strategy. But then, there is no one standard method of categorizing mutual funds. Moreover, comprehensive discussion on various types of funds is beyond the scope of this book as it can be counterproductive to our intended objectives. This is primarily because there are innumerable funds, and the fund industry offers a never-ending differentiation in its products. A comprehensive discussion on these is likely to be an overwhelming experience for most of the readers thereby defeating the very purpose of just acquainting them with the all-important big picture to empower them to fulfill their financial vision expeditiously. So here, we intend to broadly cover the basic fund types because when you grasp the requisite awareness of the basic fund types, industry's cluttered and apparently vague differentiation often clarify itself. This will empower you to decide what kind of mutual funds to buy in order to meet your investment goals.

In our opinion, the most relevant categorization of funds is the one that is derived from the asset type because it facilitates investors to find out whether a particular fund goes well with their planned asset allocation. That is why, here, the classification of funds is somewhat analogous to the investment avenues discussed in the chapter "The Investing Universe: Understanding Asset Classes." Typically, the fund name suggests the asset type or types wherein the bulk of the investment is made. Equity, debt, real estate, commodities, artwork, precious metals, etc. funds invest bulk of their kitty respectively in these assets. For instance, a real estate mutual fund seeks investors desirous of investing in a pool that will invest mainly in the real property.

Some funds invest in more than one asset category to offer solutions that are more comprehensive. There are numerous such blends offering quite a lot of permutations and combinations. Some funds also present a variable approach in which investments shift from one asset category to another depending on the market conditions and market levels to derive some extra benefit from the market volatility. In addition, sector funds offer different subsets within the main asset type to present a more focused solution to the discerning investors. Then there are thematic funds, which invest in a bouquet of sectors woven by a common theme. The range of mutual funds is only limited by the imagination of investors. And each has different attributes and different risks and rewards. Generally, the higher the risk of loss, the higher the expected return.

In spite of mixed performance and mind-boggling range, more and more people are flocking to invest in mutual funds, especially from the popular financial sector. Important funds from this sector can be grouped into three main categories, viz., Equity Funds, Debt Funds and Balanced Funds. Equity funds invest a major portion of their corpus in stocks and debt funds invest predominantly in fixed return instruments. Balanced funds provide a desired blend of growth and security by investing in both equities and fixed income instruments corresponding to the fund's objectives. The ratio of equity and debt investments influences the returns and the risks associated with the balanced funds— in case equity investments have a higher percentage, investors would be exposed to risks similar to equity to that extent. Here is a sample list of some popular fund types from both equity and debt domain.

Common Equity and Debt Fund Categories

Equity Funds	Debt Funds
• Growth Equity Funds • Value Equity Funds • Large Cap Funds • Mid Cap Funds • Small Cap Funds • Income Funds • Capital Gain Funds • Sector specific Funds • Thematic Funds • Country Funds • Region specific Funds • Global Funds • Diversified Funds • Tax- advantaged Funds • Index Funds	• Govt. Securities Funds • Corporate Bonds Funds • High Yield Bond Funds • Quality Bond Funds • Short-Term Bond Funds • Money Market Funds • Monthly Income Plans • Tax-benefit Bond Funds • Taxable Bond Funds • Fixed Income Growth Funds • Fixed Income Distribution Funds • International Bond Funds • Liquid Funds

By definition, balanced funds provide a combination of equity and debt securities to conservative investors with medium risk profile. But nowadays some of these funds offer best of the both asset classes to aggressive investors as well. Such funds are mandated to switch to any extent into equity or debt depending on the market conditions. Well-informed investors recognize that equity markets do not behave as we expect them to, and one cannot accurately predict peaks and bottoms in the roller-coaster world of equities. Market swings present an opportunity to derive some extra benefit from the volatility of the equity markets. A prudent investor, who prefers to keep his investments mainly in the financial instruments, understands the fact that in the volatile financial markets, sometimes it pays to be predominantly invested in the equity and at other times, it makes sense to shift some investments to the debt instruments. But timing the market is a very daunting task and it may not be so easy for a retail investor to decide when to make the swap. Secondly, he may not have the requisite wherewithal to execute it swiftly and cost-effectively. In such a situation, he can opt for a balanced mutual fund, which has similar objectives and a good track record of identifying market trends in time. Balanced mutual funds offer many such hybrid funds with varying degrees of risk-return trade-offs with the aim of catering to all sorts of investors.

Investors, who desire to expand their investment universe to any of the asset category discussed in the "Investing Universe" chapter but are not inclined to assume the responsibility of investing directly, can take part in their chosen asset category through the mutual fund route. They can take exposure in any asset class like real estate, precious metals, commodities or artworks using fund route that takes away the botheration of selecting and monitoring individual investments. This way they can reap the benefits of a truly diversified portfolio with the least efforts. Further, these funds facilitate investors to invest in a broad spectrum of investments from that asset class and hence, reduce investment specific risks. The mutual fund route offers an efficient and sensible alternative to an uninitiated investor to participate even in unfamiliar asset classes.

In addition to the primary categorization of the mutual funds based on the asset type, it is also imperative to become conversant with some other important fund types to get the complete picture. Mutual funds are also categorized as active and passive mutual funds. Active funds work on the premise that higher value can be found by actively and astutely managing the fund's kitty to beat the benchmark, i.e., a better performance then the opted index. In contrast, passive funds do not attempt to outperform the market, but just seek to replicate the benchmark performance. They emphasize to minimize the efforts and costs involved in managing the portfolio. All the abovementioned funds except the last line of the table are active mutual funds. Index funds and Exchange traded funds are the examples of passive funds. Now we briefly explore some interesting active and passive funds.

Lifecycle Funds

Lifecycle funds are primarily designed to enable an independent living in retirement. These funds are similar to retirement plans. That is why they are also known as target date funds. Investors can pick a lifecycle fund based on their retirement objectives and the target date of retirement. Lifecycle funds typically combine a number of strategies in a single product and follow the 'fund of funds' tactic to fulfill diverse goals. Usually, these funds allocate their corpus to a mix of underlying funds and other investments depending on the required risk-return equation. Their portfolio becomes gradually more conservative as the target date approaches. In essence, they follow the age-old practice of shifting portfolio to fixed return products in line with the stages of lifecycle. They are increasingly becoming popular as they offer single product solution for planning finances for later years. Further, lifecycle funds encourage investors to take responsibility for their financial needs in retirement. They are regarded as the future of retirement planning because of their simplicity and all-encompassing approach. However, it may not be so easy to compare them, as they are so varied and dissimilar. Furthermore, their performance cannot be compared with clear-cut yardsticks, as is the case with the most other mutual funds.

Hedge Funds

Hedging means managing risks, particularly investment risks in our context. Hedge funds were originally conceived for managing investment risks, such as market risk, interest rate risk, inflation risk, industry risk and the rest. But over a period of time, the majority of hedge funds have evolved as hyperactive funds opting for any aggressive strategy to maximize returns in addition to keeping an eye on various risk factors. No wonder that many financial experts prefer to label contemporary hedge funds as hyperactive funds. Hedge funds have their share of advantages and disadvantages.

A hedge fund is a skill based investment avenue where objective is to preserve capital and maximize returns irrespective of the investment climate. By definition, the key objective of a hedge fund is to evolve a defensive mechanism against bad times in order to deliver positive returns under all market conditions. While in practice, they attempt to do much more than just hedging. They are always on the lookout for opportunities to maximize returns. They aim to generate positive returns in both rising and falling markets. They follow a very flexible approach to investing that enables them to buy, sell, trade, use derivatives, and participate in any other investment option to take advantage of market volatility and other opportunities. Hedge funds generally go after short-term investment strategies more willingly than taking a very long-term view of the market. Hedge funds are by design adept at mitigating the risks associated with investments as well as making the most of market opportunities in their endeavor of creating wealth.

The contemporary hedge funds often use leveraging to exploit any investment avenue where they anticipate favorable risk-reward ratio. Leveraged investing is a very dangerous approach, especially considering that these funds are lightly regulated and quite flexible in their approach. Usually hedge funds give flexible mandate to the fund manager, who is invariably a deft and well-informed investment professional, to capitalize on opportunities from a broad spectrum of investment avenues to deliver equity like returns with debt like risks. In general, hedge funds have impressive record of accomplishments barring the last few years wherein they underperformed the typical long only funds as well as equity markets. A major part of their performance can be attributed to the market inefficiencies and other ingenious tricks espoused by these funds. Unfortunately, much of these gains were at the expense of other retail investors.

Hedge funds typically suit large, seasoned investors since minimum investments are large, and they charge high fees without any performance assurance. Also their risk-return equilibrium is usually on the higher side. Further, mutual funds beat hedge funds in respect of liquidity, transparency and regulations. Hence, potential hedge fund investors need to proceed with caution and avoid allocating a significant portion of their capital to this category. Succinctly, it is better to shun the temptations of hedge funds until they become credibly transparent and regulated.

Structured Products

Structured products are customized products that comprise several investments such as equity, bonds, debentures and commodities in one fund. Such funds also use options, futures and other derivatives to provide capital security and/or capital appreciation. They are designed to provide highly customized risk-return objectives and other value-added features to discerning investors.

There are many different types of structured products available in the market. Some structured products offer partial or full capital protection, depending on the fund's objectives. Structured products generally offer a pre-packaged investment strategy that is based on multiple investment instruments and many investing tactics. They often use a blend of investment strategies with varying degree of leverage and dynamic allocation, and thus making the product somewhat complex and incomparable. While structured products bring many benefits of diversification and derivatives to investors, it is better to avoid these if one does not fully understand the product under consideration. Moreover, it is often difficult for an average investor to align her or his investment objectives with these complex products.

Arbitrage Funds

The dynamics of volatile assets like equities and commodities makes it a tough game to guess the direction of the markets. It is a dicey game, as there are chances to gamble away your capital if your calls go wrong. But then, this excessive volatility offers an opportunity to make good money with no incidental risks. Arbitrage funds essentially aim to make the most of this opportunity.

Arbitraging is neither a speculation nor an investment. Arbitraging implies making gains due to volatility or market imperfections. It is a kind of trading activity intended to capture slight differences in the prices without taking either buy or sell side position. For example, whenever arbitrage fund finds a variation in the price of an investment on two different markets, it concurrently buys at the lower price and sells at the higher price to pocket the difference. Therefore, these funds are effectively hyperactive funds with a passive, investment neutral strategy.

Principal Protected Funds

The objective of principal protected funds or capital protected funds is to protect the original capital over the life of the fund. Generally, they do not seek to maximize returns by actively investing in the volatile instruments, but simply emphasize on the preservation of the capital. To achieve this objective, they usually invest the lion's share of the corpus in the secured debt instruments. This investment along with the assured returns on it over the life of the fund equalizes the original kitty of the fund, which enables the fund to guarantee capital protection. They often invest the remainder capital in high-return high-risk kind of investments in an attempt to reward the investors.

Nowadays, many capital-protected funds do not restrict their investing universe mainly to debt instruments; rather, they seek to generate good returns through active investing. Many of these funds seek to insulate the investments from the vagaries of the volatile and risky markets by using methodologies such as dynamic hedge, static hedge, dynamic portfolio insurance and constant proportion portfolio insurance.

However, the capital-protected funds do not promise to protect the purchasing power of investments, which is central to investing. They often play with the mentality of the risk-averse investors to garner more business. Many of these are just balanced funds with the largest part of investments in debt instruments. Investors should not go by the impressive names. They must read the fine print and do their own calculations in order to see these funds in the right light.

Index Funds

An index fund is meant to invest only in the assets that are part of the applicable index. All investments are maintained in the same proportion as that of the index in an attempt to match the performance of the relevant index accurately. These are passively managed funds, which merely aim to deliver returns in proportion to the related benchmark index. Index funds charge less management fees and/or commissions, as they do not require any stock-picking research or active trading facilities. They just need to replicate the yardstick index. Whenever the composition of the applicable index changes, the fund is supposed to trade just to realign its investments with the revised weightage of index constituents. Most of the time index funds deliver returns in line with the pertinent index except for the tracking errors, which are usually insignificant in the range of - 1 to +1 percentage of the corpus.

Index funds, predictably, have very low operating costs and very low turnover. Their managers are supposed to track the benchmark indices blindly. On the other hand, actively managed funds expect that their managers can outperform the benchmark indices by picking the winning stocks. Surprisingly, actually index funds outperform more than half of the actively managed funds even before considering the transaction costs difference.

The popularity of index funds may be relatively new but not their origin, which dates back to 1976 when the Vanguard group in the USA introduced the first index fund. These funds provide a superior option in the uncertain and volatile markets to the seasoned as well as the uninitiated investors who intend to capitalize on market swings. They also provide an excellent opportunity to investors who are bullish on the market but do not have requisite time or expertise to pick the individual investments. Further, the investors are not required to closely monitor the performance of index funds because their risk-return positioning is as per the relevant index.

Exchange Traded Funds

Exchange Traded Funds are not strictly mutual funds, yet they provide many of the benefits of mutual funds. They are similar to index funds and offer the same advantages as they also represent a basket of investments. An exchange-traded fund (ETF) is usually traded on an exchange like a share, and the market forces determine the price of the ETF. And the net asset value is irrelevant in the context of ETF. They are as liquid as common stocks. They are also economical to trade because investor is not required to pay any management fees or entry/exit loads except for the commission payable to the broker. By buying an ETF, the investor is effectively buying all the constituents of that ETF in the same proportion as represented in the fund. So, they are analogous to an index fund with consequential benefits of diversification and passive investment strategy.

The popularity of these funds is continually increasing ever since they were introduced. These funds are very useful for both small and large investors, as they provide all the benefits of diversification without the associated groundwork. They are excellent tools to invest in the specific sectors of the economy, including physical assets, where investors have an optimistic view of the future performance. Investors, who have strong views on some sectors of the market, which may be inconsistent with their assessment of the overall market trend, can make the most of these funds by initiating conflicting positions as per their assessment. Nearly all these funds permit intra day trading. Many of these also provide the facility to buy or sell on margins. Mutual funds cannot offer this type of flexibility and low expenses. The ETFs are becoming the preferred choice of mature and cost conscious investors despite the insignificant promotion of the ETFs in comparison to the mutual funds. When many mutual funds are not outperforming their benchmarks, the very model of active mutual funds looks shaky, especially considering the low cost alternatives like index funds and exchange traded funds.

Yet, another way of categorizing all funds is derived from their structure. Mutual funds can also be categorized based on their structure in open-end mutual funds and close-end mutual funds.

Open-End Mutual Funds

Open-end mutual funds are the most familiar and common category of mutual funds. Open-end funds allow investors to buy and sell the shares at any point of time at the market determined current NAV (net assets value is calculated by dividing the current value of the fund's assets by the number of its existing shares). Open-end funds operate in a dynamic way since market capitalization of the assets under fund's management is continually changing as new investors join in and existing ones pull out. Affordability and convenience make these funds most popular of the lot considering the small lot sizes and liquidity advantages. This is why more and more investors are parking their incremental savings in the performance oriented open-end funds.

Close-End Mutual Funds

A close end mutual fund sells a specified number of shares at an initial public offering and normally sells no additional shares after that. Usually the price of a share of a close end fund is not ascertained as per NAV of the fund but is determined by the demand and supply of the shares in the market. So, close-end funds may trade at a premium or discount to their NAV. The trading of these shares usually bears a resemblance to the trading of common equity shares. Accordingly, their prices fluctuate in accordance with the market forces of demand and supply in addition to the performance of the fund. Characteristically, these funds are long-term and stable because their corpus is more or less fixed. Generally, the close-end funds intend to capitalize on the long-term direction of the market and typically provide some leeway and time to the fund manager to perform as stated by the schedule and mandate of the fund.

Many mutual funds offer a choice of investment plans in order to cater to different investor needs. Investors can select a plan on the basis of their profile and investment goals. The track record of the mutual fund's scheme is also an important consideration in finalizing an investment plan. Here are some of the important fund plans.

Growth Plan aims to retain the gains made by the fund in order to provide for capital appreciation. The advantage of this plan is that the dividends or any other income simply accumulate in the net asset value of the fund, and the investor need not bother about looking for alternative investment avenues for incremental income. Growth plans suit aggressive and long-term investors because power of compounding works in favor of these plans.

Dividend Plan or Income Plan invariably provides regular income to investors, which demonstrates its capacity to generate steady gains to payout the investors. After payout, the total corpus of the fund goes down by the dividend/income paid out and so does the net assets value of the fund. Accordingly, these funds exhibit lesser tendency to fall during bearish phases and are the preferred choice of risk-averse and retired investors.

Dividend Re-investment Plan gives an option to investors to automatically reinvest the dividend or income declared in the fund through purchase of fresh shares at the prevailing net assets value. As a result, investors' holding in terms of number of shares will go on increasing with each payout. Generally, investors have a choice to receive income or reinvest the same in the same fund. Investors usually opt for the reinvestment option, especially when the fund is performing well so as to capitalize on this plus point over and above the benefits of power of compounding.

Systematic Investment Plan gives the option to invest a fixed sum every month instead of deploying finances at one go. This plan allots shares to the participating investors at the applicable NAVs on the day of the respective payments. This way the investors need not take the risk of timing the market. SIP is a staggered approach to investing that takes care of the cost-averaging concept of investing as well as inculcates regular savings habit. SIP particularly suits monthly income earners. The conservative investors are increasingly opting for the SIP way of investing to take advantage of cost averaging, draw on the concept of time value of money and to sidestep the problem of market timing.

Systematic Withdrawal Plan gives an option to the investors to withdraw a fixed sum or redeem pre-determined units every month or at a pre-defined interval. Withdrawal amount is calculated at the applicable NAV as on the day of redemption. This plan is designed for regular income seekers and retirees.

Normally, the fund's title and description indicate the objectives as well as suggest the likely investment portfolio of the scheme. But investors must acquaint themselves with all the highlights as well as the finer points so as to make sure that they not only buy the right fund, but also continue with a well-balanced and dependable portfolio of investments. Investors cannot solely depend on the fund advisors to ensure that they actually get what they really want. They need to pay the due attention and devote some time to explore their mutual funds investment options before committing. In the next chapter, we shall discuss how to select the right funds for your investment portfolio.

4.3 Choosing Funds: Separating the Best from the Rest

Investors today are spoilt for options when it comes to choosing a mutual fund. Markets are inundated with perplexing variety of funds, each offering something special to attract investors. With thousands of mutual funds in the market, each proclaiming to take care of the investor's objectives, the task of picking a few to include in your portfolio can be overwhelming, especially for tyros. Investors opt for mutual funds primarily because they find it difficult to choose specific investments independently owing to the endless choices with varying degrees of risks. But then, due to the vast number of mutual funds where each one is proclaiming to cater to the investor's needs, choosing a few funds may not be any easier. Investors are in a fix. And the problem of plenty is the cause of their plight.

Moreover, one could not be expected to remain impervious to all the media hype generated by good and bad fund offerings, particularly in the absence of a suitable framework to evaluate the fund schemes. Further, to make the matter more obscure, there is the incessant flow of newer varieties offering more and more features. For instance, a mutual fund commonly referred to as the 'fund of funds' is often promoted as a better and all-inclusive solution. Investors should not seek solace in new and alluring products as it remains to be seen how newer offerings, such as structures products or fund of funds that are essentially a concoction of other funds, perform relative to other established fund types. Secondly, they are likely to muddle up investor' desirable asset allocation, which is the vital element of their investment planning.

It is quite common that unscrupulous fund agents deliberately promote a scheme, which may not be consistent with the investor's goals but makes a great deal for the sellers. Further, investors must keep in mind that distributors enjoy enormous clout because of their indispensable role in the fiercely competitive world of mutual funds. Considering this and to gain from the fund investments in the chosen asset category, investors need to take well-informed and carefully considered investment decisions before committing their money to any fund.

Many investors blindly rely on the advice of investment consultants to select mutual funds. They should understand the fund selection process adopted by the consultants before committing their capital. Some people tend to follow tips from friends or go by the media hype in an impulsive manner, thereby making their investments susceptible to various risks. Instead of following the herd, you need to create your own mechanism to identify the fund investments that are in line with your financial goals. This carefully planned framework will help you to select the right funds in a dispassionate manner, and persist with your investment plan regardless of popular opinion.

Amidst all this push and pull, let us examine how you should go about selecting the right fund. Here our objective is to devise a simple framework to enable an uninitiated investor to pick a fund wherein investment objectives most closely match her or his own goals. The fund route proves to be a really rewarding experience for investors who diligently clarify their personal investment goals before selecting a mutual fund. If you want to get the most out of your fund investments, the next important step is to look at the credentials of various funds under consideration as well as whether they align with your personal investment objectives. Accordingly, our fund selection framework comprises of two segments, viz. personal issues and funds' factors.

Let us begin by appreciating the personal issues that play a vital role in identifying the right mutual funds as well as to maintain an optimal portfolio. First, we take the key question to facilitate a clear and deep perception of the situation. *Why you should prefer mutual funds over direct investing?*

Your investing needs are as unique as you are. So, you should brainstorm over this question for sometime to put your unique investing needs in the right perspective. Here, we give some examples of the many reasons that may justify assigning a reasonable share of your investments to the mutual funds.

> ➢ You are not proficient in the investment category wherein you wish to invest.
> ➢ You cannot spare time and/or lack monitoring skills to keep tabs on your investments.
> ➢ You may not be good enough at timing the markets. (picking near bottoms and quitting near peaks)
> ➢ Can you manage the transition- requiring a shift in the mindset from self-indulgence to self-denial?
> ➢ You wish to have a benchmark to compare your performance.
> ➢ You cannot participate directly due to the large ticket sizes.
> ➢ You are susceptible to become possessive and emotional about your investments.
> ➢ You find an investment avenue too hot to suit your temperament but it appears to be a potentially rewarding opportunity.
> ➢ You wish to attune yourself to a new investment category or to a new market before investing directly.

After mulling over your personal triggers that persuade you to choose funds in your investment plan, you can start your category identification process with reference to your asset allocation table wherein you can incorporate two columns for allocating proportion between direct investment and mutual fund route against each asset class. Before stipulating investment ratio on the side of mutual funds, it is desired that you clarify your investment criteria for that particular asset class. You can help yourself with the standard investment criteria tables discussed while evaluating various asset classes. Careful analysis of these investment criteria tables can give you an idea whether to go for the fund route as well as decide the optimal allocation for the fund investments. What this means is that you can easily determine the tentative percentages of fund investments for each category of assets by considering your personal issues relative to that category. This is illustrated in the following sample table to help you get the practical picture.

Asset Allocation: Direct vs. Fund Investments Worksheet
(Percentage)

Investment Type	Allocation %	Direct Investment	Fund Investment
Real Estate:			
i.House	Excluded	NA	NA
ii.Investments	10	10	0
Equity:			
i.Growth stocks	15	5	10
ii.Value stocks	25	10	15
Fixed Income:			
i.Bonds	10	5	5
ii.Treasury Bills	10	10	0
Commodities	10	0	10
Artworks	5	0	5
Precious Metals	10	10	0
Cash/Cash like	5	5	NA

After determining the share of fund investments in your asset allocation table, the next step is to explore the appropriate options available in the specific domains. Each fund pursues a pre-defined set of objectives, making it workable for the investors to compare their investment goals with the objectives of fund. This way, in theory, the investors can certainly align their investment needs with the funds' investment philosophy. But with a vast and often overwhelming range of funds to choose from, separating the probable winners from the rest is not a simple task. In spite of that, it is imperative to sift through the lot to find out the cream of the crop. Therefore, with the aim of facilitating investors to take well-informed investment decisions, we are enumerating here the important factors to be considered while evaluating a fund scheme.

> - Fund's Philosophy
> - Relative Benchmark
> - Management Team
> - Investment Strategy
> - Diversification Level
> - Time of Launch
> - Portfolio Holdings
> - Annualized Fees and Expenses
> - Tax Benefits, if any
> - Size of the Kitty
> - Past Performance, if any
> - Annual Portfolio Turnover
> - Cash Flows/ Liquidity Aspects
> - Risk Disclosures

By moving through these stages, you can ensure that you get your hands on the potential winners. This hands-on process will make sure that your money works harder and smarter for you. In addition, you will be sure of your investments and stay poised even in the roller-coaster movements of the market. However, in case you find the fund selection process somewhat overwhelming you can seek advice from an independent investment professional. Alternatively, you may help yourself to a basic analytical technique catering to your concerns along the lines of the following blueprint. Remember, you are now in a position to decide on the basis of your own opinion, not those of others, the important and pertinent factors to be considered for evaluating the short listed funds. You may perhaps prefer to assign suitable weights to the factors in order to get a dispassionate and logical result. Alternatively, you may use different degrees of 'Suitable...Not Suitable' against each factor to keep it somewhat subjective and rational process.

Mutual Funds Evaluation Table

Selection Criteria	Weight	Fund 1	Fund 2	Fund 3
Personal Issues:				
Fund Factors:				
Total	100			

The above analysis will help you to resolve which funds to select and which funds to ignore. Though it has its own flaws, it offers a very convenient technique for choosing the funds that may be right for you. One obvious limitation of this simple analysis is that it pays no heed to the market forces that ultimately determine the asset prices at a particular point of time. At times, media hype and rumor mills exaggerate some issues to the extent that it induces the man-made pressures on demand or supply thereby creating a mismatch. This created mismatch is essentially temporary in nature because the false perceptions, hype and rumors have a short life. But this mismatch along with our herd instincts can take the prices to artificial levels in the near term owing to artificial imbalances created by all-around pressure on the demand or supply. In this way, occasionally speculators and people with herd mentality can make quick gains. However, you should ignore the popular opinion when that is contrary to your well thought-out investing decisions.

Most investors hardly find enough time to research, select and monitor what could be the best investments for their portfolio. The concerns of busy investors are well addressed by passively investing through mutual funds, which can effectively meet most of their investment needs across all asset classes. But they must keep in mind that even passive participation requires not only the initial study to separate the best from the rest, but also demands the periodic reviews of their valuable assets. These periodic reviews help you to evaluate whether your investments are working as hard as envisaged; besides, they provide a chance to contemplate a change in your strategies when they are not working as anticipated. The timely reviews also enable you to resort to new measures to cash in on the current opportunities as well as ensure the desired returns. Remember, you can take control of your financial destiny by planning well and executing the plans even better.

At the end of the day, neither the direct investing nor the fund route is a clear winner, and earnest investors should prudently allocate appropriate share to both avenues based on their personal profile and the shrewd assessment of the asset classes.

Part 5

The Goals of Making Money

5.1 Buying a Home

Buying a home is a big investment decision with emotional strings attached. A home is one of the largest purchases most of us will ever make in our lives. And there are many benefits of buying a home, especially for first-time homebuyers. But then, some people are not cut out for home ownership, for a variety of reasons. Our needs and stage in life essentially influence the decision to buy our first home. There are many other factors that we need to consider before investing in what may be our most prized possession. Since we have already discussed real estate assets as an investment avenue in the investing universe chapter, we intend to focus on the first home purchase in this chapter.

Is a home a good investment? This is a big decision that requires a lot of groundwork, deliberations, and evaluation of the life goals. The first home is important for everyone. Yet, home ownership may not suit everyone. It is a long-term and large commitment. In addition, it is also one of the most complicated and complex investment. The asset selection decisions such as location, size, quality, price and future prospects as well as procedural decisions such as government regulations, legal jargon and numerous mortgage choices that are a part of the home purchasing process invariably require time, money and expertise to take a holistic and rational decision while acquiring this important asset.

Besides, the growth of real estate industry is very important for the economy. So, many times the governments and vested interest unduly prop up the demand in the housing market, which leads to artificially jacked-up prices in the sector. Small investors can burn their fingers during such hot periods. While realty is a real wealth creation strategy, one needs to take a well thought out decision before committing. Your first home buying decision will be much more balanced and easier to apply if you break it down into the following parts.

A. Is buying a home right for you?
  • Advantages and disadvantages of buying and renting
  • Cost-benefit comparison of buying vs. renting

B. How much can you afford to spend on a home?
  • What is the down payment you can comfortably afford?
  • What is the value range you are considering?
  • What is the mortgage component you are taking into account?

C. What type of home do you want?
  • Home comparison worksheet— House factors
  • Home comparison worksheet— Convenience factors

D. Do you understand the home loan financing process?
  • Which home loan is right for you?
  • How you can wisely compare various mortgage options on a standard scale?

Is Buying a Home Right for You?

More often than not, the first home is a greatly desired asset. Yet, the decision to buy may not be a wise option at times. In addition to your financial and personal factors, the market conditions will influence the decision to buy or rent. Extreme exuberance or severe skepticism in the housing market as well as your transferable job may discourage you to buy a home. And while the financial factors such as capital appreciation and tax benefits may prompt you to buy a home, your financial constraints may induce you to rent a home.

Is it better to buy or rent? No one can say for sure which option is better. Whether buying is better than renting depends on many factors. Buying a home, in the financial context, is the right choice if rents and home prices both go up in future. And if they both go down, renting is a better choice. Depending on your personal circumstances and market conditions, both buying and renting have advantages and disadvantages. Here we briefly outline some of these.

Advantages of buying a home:

✓ Property builds equity as value appreciates. You can borrow against equity
✓ Pride of homeownership as well as sense of community, stability, and security
✓ Can be a form of forced savings (repayment of a loan) and potential for capital gain due to increase in market value
✓ Free to change decor and landscaping
✓ Tax benefits on mortgage interest and property taxes
✓ A home has historically been a hedge against inflation
✓ You can upgrade your home as you see fit.

Disadvantages of buying a home:
? Often a home purchase reduces flexibility and liquidity of the investment portfolio. In many cases, it skews the portfolio with a large chunk that is somewhat illiquid
? Possibility of foreclosure and loss of equity
? Responsible for property taxes
? Less mobility than renting. Relocating will involve substantial time and money. May have to wait until market conditions are right
? You pay for all utilities, property taxes and insurance
? Responsible for property maintenance
? Home improvement upgrades can cost quite a bundle.

Advantages of renting a home:
✓ Little or no responsibility for maintenance, property taxes, insurance, etc.
✓ Easier to move without major time or money costs
✓ No concern about foreclosure if income changes
✓ Capital not tied up in the home, and available for other uses
✓ You are not financially responsible for improvements.

Disadvantages of renting a home:
? No equity is built up. Your money goes toward the landlord's equity
? No chance for capital gain
? No control over rent increases
? No ownership. You need permission to make any changes

? Security deposit and other initial expenses may be required. Return of security deposit may be subject to property owner's discretion

? No tax benefits.

After appreciating the pros and cons of the buying vs. renting decision in a somewhat subjective manner, now you need to evaluate it rationally on the basis of cost benefit analysis. Potential for capital appreciation and savings are important indicators. After all building wealth is the most important consideration for an investor. You can use the following table to compare your costs and savings in both the options.

Buying Vs. Renting: Cost-Benefit Comparison

Costs and Savings	Buying ($)	Renting ($)
A. Annual Expenses:		
Mortgage		NA
Annual Rent	NA	
Maintenance		NA
Insurance		
Property Taxes		NA
Annual Expenses Total A =		
B. Savings and Gains:		
Principal repaid on mortgage		NA
Tax Savings		NA
Return on down payment @... %	NA	
Property Appreciation @... %		NA
Annual Savings & Gains Total B =		
Annual Net Cost (A-B) =		

The rent is likely to increase every year whereas the amount due as the mortgage repayment may remain somewhat fixed. Property appreciation in the above example is a very important component and varies significantly. Occasionally, homebuyers can also experience decrease in the market value of the property. But then, tax savings are available only to homebuyers and are more significant for those in high tax brackets. Homebuyers do not earn any return on the money spent on the down payment and other costs; therefore, the return lost on that money is included as a savings to renters. Prospective buyers should compare the above cost-benefit analysis at least for five years before taking any decision.

Even if you decide that buying a home is not the right choice for you, you should keep this option open for future. Sometimes, market forces or your personal factors may discourage you to invest in the housing, and home ownership may not be the right decision now, but most probably, you will require your own home in future. And remember that historical data proves that realty is a real wealth creation avenue in the long run. So, you should explore ways to build equity for home even if you prefer renting right now. While exploring various asset classes in the investment universe chapter, you have seen that one can expect capital appreciation as well as rental income from the real estate investments.

How Much Can You Afford?

Homeownership is supposed to make you feel settled and secure, and that includes financially. After deciding to buy your first home, you should examine your finances so as to decide how much you can easily afford as down payment as well as mortgage payment per month. Since you pay for your home with a combination of a down payment and a home loan, the total of both is the price you can afford to pay for your home. Based on your investments that you are willing to put into your house, you can easily figure out the down payment part. However, keep in mind that the down payment part should ideally be at least 20% of the purchase price to get better mortgage terms. To help you easily calculate an affordable down payment, we give hereunder a worksheet that you can complete with the help of your summarized personal financial status prepared while evaluating your financial health.

Deciding a Reasonable Down Payment

Description	Amount	Amount
A. Funds Available:		
Net Equity		
Net Bonds, etc.		
Net Commodities		
Net Mutual Funds		
Insurance-Net Value		
Net Misc. Investments/ Savings		
Net Equity in present home		
Less: Contingency Reserves		
Funds Available	Total A	+
B. Expenses Anticipated:		
Settlement Costs		
Repairs & Renovation		
Furnishing Costs		
Shifting Expenses		
Other Misc. Expenses		
Expenses Anticipated	Total B	-
Funds Available for Down Payment	A-B	

As a rule of thumb, you can afford to spend two and half (2.5) times your annual gross income on your home. If you earn

$200,000 per annum, you can typically afford a home worth $500,000. This is a very rough estimate and the actual numbers will vary based on what you can spend comfortably for your monthly housing expenses. Lenders will also consider other factors like current interest rates, your debt and credit history.

Mortgage lenders typically use Housing Expense Ratio and Debt-to-Income Ratio to determine how much you can afford to spend on your monthly mortgage payment. Housing expense ratio is the percentage of your gross monthly income that goes towards the monthly mortgage payments including principal, interest, taxes and insurance. Preferably, this ratio should be 28% or lower, but this percentage can change based on the type of mortgage you choose.

The debt to income ratio is calculated by dividing your total monthly debt payments by your gross monthly income before taxes are deducted. This ratio is a standard tool for assessing whether a borrower will have difficulty meeting her or his repayment obligations. Preferably, this ratio should be 36% or lower, but this percentage can vary based on your personal factors and the prevailing money market conditions.

However, the most important factor in deciding how much you can afford is taking an honest look at what you can spare for your monthly housing expenses based on your income and other expenses. So, you should review the following to determine how much you can comfortably afford on housing every month.

» Income,
» Savings,
» Monthly expenses, and
» Debt.

Analyzing the above factors in the context of your monthly income and expense account will help you determine how big a loan you can afford as well as how buying a home will affect your monthly budget. Remember that you should consider how much you want to pay each month for housing based on your personal budget and not on the basis of biggest mortgage a lender qualifies you to borrow. You can use the following table to estimate your qualifying mortgage amount based on your monthly housing expenses, i.e., monthly principal, interest payment, etc.

Calculating a Monthly Mortgage

Loan Rate	Cost Per $1,000
5.00%	5.37
5.50%	5.68
6.00%	6.00
6.25%	6.16
6.50%	6.32
6.75%	6.49
7.00%	6.65
7.25%	6.83
7.50%	6.99
7.75%	7.17
8.00%	7.34
8.50%	7.69

To calculate the monthly principal and interest payments on a $100,000 loan at 5 % for conventional 30 years mortgage, multiply $5.37 by 100 (100x $5.37) to get $537. When deciding what you can afford, you should look at the big picture and not just the price of the home. Remember that the mortgage is not the only expense of homeownership. You should also consider other expenses such as maintenance costs, taxes, utilities, homeowner's insurance and unexpected repairs.

You can also use your rent to determine your comfortable monthly mortgage payment. Since you can avail tax benefits of homeownership, you can roughly afford to pay 30% more than your current rent payment as housing expenses. So, you can just multiply your rent by 1.3 to determine your housing loan repayment potential.

You can also use the following equation to calculate your monthly mortgage payment @ 28% loan ratio, and then use it to check your maximum mortgage eligibility with reference to mortgage calculators or tables.

Monthly mortgage payment = [(Gross monthly income x 0.28) – Monthly taxes and insurance on the home]

What Type of Home Do You Want?

After considering *why* you should buy a home and *what* you can afford, now is the time to explore *when, where* and *what* kind of home you want to buy. Here, we are talking about a home, not a house. So, you must also consider your family's preferences while deciding your dream home. Remember, a house is made of walls and beams; a home is built with love and dreams.

While exploring your home, bear in mind that home purchase is a long-term commitment. So, you should also consider your future requirements, or else you may find later that you have outgrown it. There are a lot of things to keep in mind in order to make an informed decision. You need to think about the following questions before making your home selection worksheet.

» Where (what part of country) do you want to live in?
» What size do you prefer (square feet)?
» How many bedrooms & bathrooms would you like to have?
» When you want to move in your new home?
» What is your preferred price range?
» What kind of houses would you be willing to see?
» Do you prefer an older home or a new home?
» Do you have any animals that will require special facilities?
» Do you have to be close to public transportation?
» How much renovation would you be willing to do?
» What features do you want to have in your house?

Usually people look at many houses before finding the one that suits them. All the efforts are worth it given that many of them are making the single largest investment of their life. But then, choosing a house is a complex and tricky process owing to various factors. Many times buyers go out with stars in their eyes and buy with emotions rather than with their minds. Their subjective and irrational comparisons lead to wrong decisions, which buyers regret later.

While choosing a home, it is important to reign in your emotions and concentrate on what is really important. You should not let your emotions override a rational assessment of whether a particular house really meets your needs. Here we give a comparison checklist to help you easily evaluate your choices.

Home Comparison Worksheet— House Factors

The House Factors	# ABC	#XYZ
Location- address		
Size (square feet)		
Price		
Yearly expenses (maintenance, taxes, etc.)		
Style of house		
Number of bedrooms		
Number of bathrooms		
Interior condition		
Storage space		
Basement condition (dampness, smell, etc.)		
Exterior condition		
Roof condition		
Garage /Lawn/Yard space/Fence		
Appliances		
Others		

Home Comparison Worksheet— Convenience Factors

The Convenience Factors	# ABC	#XYZ
Schools		
Traffic		
Noise Level		
Neighborhood- average age, nature, etc.		
Safety/Security		
Public transportation		
Airport		
Shopping		
Hospital		
Restaurants/entertainment		
Recreation/parks		
Others		

Do You Understand the Home Loan Financing Process?

When selecting a home loan, it pays to figure out what you want from your home loan and how much it will cost you. The home loan market is very big and competitive market. There are several types of mortgage lenders such as commercial banks, mortgage companies and thrift institutions in the home loans market, each offering a wide range of loans with different interest rates, product features and fees. So, before deciding which loan type to choose and from which lender, it is important to explore the market and compare options. This will not only help you find the loan that fits your needs and wants, but will also save you some money every month.

Comparing only the interest rates or equated monthly installments will not help you to take the right decision. You should find out all the terms and conditions as well as the components of your monthly home loan repayment. In order to compare the information in a meaningful way, try to get information about the same loan amount, loan term, and type of loan. You must ask for the following information from each mortgage lender.

- A list of its current mortgage interest rates under various schemes
- The lender's requirements for a down payment
- Whether the rate is variable or fixed or partially-fixed
- Estimates of fees such as underwriting fees, broker fees, transaction settlement and closing costs. Demand an explanation of any fee you do not understand
- What is the estimated insurance cost
- Confirm the loan's annual percentage rate that takes into account not only the interest rate but also points, broker fees, and other fees & charges that you may be required to pay, expressed as a yearly rate
- Check about any special offers.

Types of Mortgages

When exploring various types of home loans, it is very important to pick the one that fits your needs and circumstances. While there are many different types of mortgages, but they all have a few features in common:

- There is an approval process, where you need to prove to the lender that you are a credit worthy borrower and can afford to repay the loan.
- You usually have to contribute partly in the cost of your house.
- Your loan is secured by your house. While it entitles you to a lower rate of interest, your lender has the right to sell your house to get his money back if you do not repay as agreed.

Most people prefer a standard home loan wherein you make regular payments against the principal and interest. This type of loan allows you to slowly but surely repay your home loan because regular repayments mean you are gradually reducing the loan amount. Loan tenor is usually an agreed time, such as 15 or 20 years. Variable rate, fixed rate and partially-fixed rate loans are popular variants of standard home loans.

Variable rate home loans are also known as adjustable rate mortgages (ARMs) or floating rate loans. The interest rate is not fixed in this type of loan. The interest rate is usually linked to an economic index, and your repayments are periodically adjusted up or down as the index changes. The purpose of the interest rate adjustments is primarily to bring the interest rate on the loan at the level of market rates. Homebuyers prefer this type of loan because it usually has lower initial interest rates than fixed rate mortgages.

A fixed rate home loan has a pre-determined, fixed interest rate for an agreed period of time. The fixed rate mortgage offers you the security of knowing exactly what your repayments will be for the duration of your home loan. They are well suited to long term budgetary planning and peace of mind as a result of the stability of the payments.

As the name suggests, a partially-fixed rate home loan is a combination of both fixed and variable rates. In this type of loan, borrowers should be very clear about how the principal and interest repayments are worked out. Many permutations and combinations of fixed and variable components can help you to design your mortgage as per your needs and considerations. Here also your repayments still fluctuate, but will not vary as much as a variable loan since you get some advantages of a fixed loan and some advantages of a variable loan.

In addition to the above-mentioned common home loans, there are several other types of home loans such as interest-only option loans, balloon mortgage, sub prime loans, low-doc loans, vendor finance and equity release products each with different features. Then there are several types of mortgage lenders, who may have different names for some fees and may charge different interest rates, fees, etc. There can also be some variation in terminology as well as methods of calculations from lender to lender.

So, it is worth taking the time to shop around and compare the available options on a standard scale. Understanding your loan options and negotiating your home loan can save you quite a bit of money. You can use the following home loan checklist to judiciously compare your loan options.

A Home Loan Comparison Checklist

Particulars	Lender A	Lander B
Lender Details		
Type of Mortgage		
Minimum down payment required		
Loan tenure (length of loan)		
Contract interest rate		
Annual percentage rate (APR)		
Expected monthly payment(principal, interest, taxes, insurance, etc.)		
Fees and charges:		
Start up fees		
Appraisal fee		
Estimated prepaid amounts for interest, taxes, insurance, etc.		
State and local taxes, stamp duty, transfer taxes		
Other significant fees		
Features:		
Frequency of rate change for variable loan		
Prepayment penalties		
Is there a fee to lock in?		
Extra repayments terms		
Other relevant points		

It is important to understand how different mortgages may change your repayments over time. It is also equally important to have a look at your personal budget and financial status to understand which home loan is best for you in the long run.

Buying a home is not just about getting a nice place to live; it is also about your life and your dreams. And remember that it is a huge investment, and it can be an excellent wealth creation strategy owing to its twin benefits of lower interest rates and tax benefits provided that you can identify an appreciating property.

But then, like other growth assets, realty also is volatile and requires long-term orientation. In exchange for better returns, real estate often requires tolerance for risk and volatility and is not amenable to advance forecasts. However, due to easy availability of home loans, many rush to buy property without adequate planning. Thanks to ubiquitous mortgage loans, the realty dream has become a reality for many deserving as well as not-so-deserving people.

Buying a home after all the deliberations is great so long as one remembers it is not an end in itself. Realty and mortgage markets are meant to be efficient, not sufficient; aggressively competitive, not fair. So, it is good to expect the best, but equally important to be prepared for the worst. It will hold you in good stead in this game of investing.

5.2 Securing Children's Future

We want to be the best parent we can be. We all want nothing but the best for our children. We have dreams and desires for our kids and ourselves as parents. After all our children is our future. However, sometimes for lack of planning and foresight, things get in the way of us being the parent we want to be.

We all know the importance of upbringing. That is why we want our children to get the best education. We also know that good education and tech skills are becoming more and more important for a good career. The merger of globalization and infotech is driving huge productivity gains for employers who find it easier and economical to replace employees with computers, machines, robots, and foreigners. Now things are not only limited to cheap foreign labor, but cheap foreign genius is also finding many takers. Greater global competition along with shrinking job opportunities is creating a really competitive career market where good education is the key to survive and thrive.

As we are moving further into the knowledge economy, access to good education will be a crucial determinant of good life. Children's education planning is important for all, including the fortunate souls who do not foresee any financial constraints. And it is not just for the financial rewards; it also offers emotional dividends for both parent and child.

But then, there are so many indeterminate variables, such as subject choices, school and college selection, future cost of education, inflation rate, expected returns on investments, scholarship availability, future demand & supply trends and the rest, which make the financial planning for children's education a really tricky exercise. What's more, government's education funding and other policies differ not only from state to state and country to country, but also from time to time. While economy or state is not supposed to negatively impact the funding structure of the education system, but unfortunately that is not the case.

Earlier, the things were not so tricky. But now, it is not easy to predict what the future holds. Governments' dwindling budgets and educational institution's balance sheets compel them to change policies that are not good for the future of education seekers. The future appears to be more uncertain in the uncertain current situation and thus making children's education planning more imperative as well as more complex. But we cannot leave our children's future at the mercy of chance.

You can effectively deal with all these uncertainties with a structured plan and flexible approach. Your plan ought to be sufficiently flexible and adaptable to fit the unpredictable future situations. This you can achieve by making your child's education planning checklist and periodically reviewing it to keep it relevant and contemporary. Here we give a broad idea of an education-planning checklist.

1. What are your tentative education goals for your child?
    • What type of school and college do you expect your child to attend?
    • What are the school and college timelines?
    • What are the current and anticipated costs?
2. Can you finance the education expenses without savings?
    • If not, what are your savings goals?
    • If yes, whether the allocated funds are suitably invested.
3. Can you count on other sources to fund your child's education?
    • Relatives
    • Child's contribution
    • Scholarships
    • Grants, subsidies, etc.
    • Financial aid, loan, etc.
4. What is the status of your current savings for this purpose?
    • How much is the present value of your savings?
    • How your savings are invested?
    • Can you accurately predict the future value of your savings? Whether savings are invested in fixed return instruments, or their returns depend on the market forces.
    • What is the anticipated future value of your savings?
5. Are you prepared to effectively use tax and other benefits available for education?

6. What is your monthly savings cum investment strategy to provide for your child's education?

Even though it may not be possible to precisely predict many variables involved in estimating the cost of your child's education, it is important to have a plan in place. While hoping for the best from the system and the child who should be encouraged to make the most of scholarships, it is better to plan your savings and investments with the intention that you can fund your child's education on your own. It pays to be self-sufficient when it comes to the children's future planning. By having a savings plan in place, you can make it possible for your child to get the education s/he deserves. Here we illustrate how you can estimate future cost of education and then determine monthly savings required to meet your goal.

I. Calculating Expected Cost of Education: Let us look at a hypothetical example to find out future value of your child's college education. Suppose you plan to send your daughter to college in 15 years, and you have ascertained that current cost of projected college education is approximately $30,000 per year for five years, i.e., a total of $150,000. Next, you need to estimate the cost of college education 15 years from now considering inflation rate at 8%. To calculate this figure, you can use Excel or any spreadsheet program as illustrated here below.

	A	B	C
1	Present Value- $	150,000	
2	Years	15	
3	Annual Rate	8%	
4			
5	Future Value- $	475,825	=FV(B3,B2,0,-B1)

To find the future value of 150,000 (i.e. present cost), we use the FV (Future Value) function, which is defined as: FV(rate,nper,pmt,pv,type). You just need to key in the present value, years and inflation rate in cells B1, B2 and B3 respectively. Now type this formula in cell B5 =FV (B3, B2, 0,-B1) and then press Enter. The answer will be 475,825 that will be the cost of intended college education after 15 years. [You can also use fx function to know the future value. Select fx function from the Insert menu and then write FV and enter go, or choose financial category & select

FV function. In the box that appears, Rate is the inflation rate (8%), Nper is the number of periods (15) and PV is the present value (150,000). You can skip the PMT field, which is required for periodic payments, and the type field, which represents the timing of the payment.] For parents who are not all that computer savvy, a simple paper worksheet method is also illustrated next.

II. Calculating Future Value of Available Funds: Suppose that you have already saved $ 50,000 for her higher education and invested it in the fixed return instruments yielding 6% per annum return. To find out the future value of this amount, you can use the above-mentioned formula or fx function. Remember, the increases in college costs currently outpace inflation as well as returns from fixed instruments, and this trend is expected to continue. Here is your spreadsheet.

	A	B	C
1	Present Value- $	50,000	
2	Years	15	
3	Annual Rate	6%	
4			
5	Future Value- $	119,829	=FV(B3,B2,0,-B1)

III. Calculating Monthly Savings Required: Now you know the expected shortfall, i.e., future value of cost of education *less* future value of available funds (475825 – 119829 = 355996). Next, you have to find out how much money would you need to save and invest every month to achieve your goal. You expect to earn an average annual return of 5% by investing your savings in risk free instruments. Your excel formula is =PMT(B3,B2,0,B1) to calculate annual savings required to reach your goal, i.e. accumulate $ 356,000 in 15 years. You can use fx function as well to compute required annual savings.

	A	B	C
1	Future Value- $	356,000	
2	Years	15	
3	Annual Rate	5%	
4			
5	Annual Saving- $	(15,498)	=PMT(B3,B2,0,B1)
6.	Monthly Saving- $	(1375)	=B5 ÷12

Here is your consolidated spreadsheet based on the above three calculations. You can manipulate it easily by changing various variables like annual rate, costs or savings to explore the impact of various factors on your calculations. This excel sheet helps you to conveniently look into various permutations and combinations, such as optimistic view, pessimistic view, probable scholarships and tax benefits.

Excel Spreadsheet of College Education Costs & Savings

A	B
I. Calculating Expected Costs:	
Present Value- $	150000
Years	15
Annual Rate (inflation rate)	8%
Future Value	$475,825
II. Calculating Available Funds:	
Present Value- $	50000
Years	15
Annual Rate (return/yield)	6%
Future Value	$119,828
III. Calculating Monthly Savings Required:	
Future Value- (I - II)	$356,000
Years	15
Annual Rate (return/yield)	5%
Annual Saving	($16,500)
Monthly Saving Required	($1375)

However, if you wish to use paper and pen rather than Excel or any other spreadsheet, here is a simple college education cost and savings worksheet, which you can use with the help of tables of future value factors and future value of annuity factors given next.

College Education Costs & Savings Worksheet

	Amount $
A. Calculating Expected Costs:	
1. Years until your child begins college	15
2. Current annual cost of college education	30,000
3. Total college cost	150,000
(2 x no. of years in college, i.e., 5)	
4. Cost inflation factor	3.1722
(refer table F.V. below, 15years @ 8%)	
5. Future cost of college education (3x 4)	475,825
B. Calculating Available Funds:	
1. Savings available	50,000
2. Future value factor	
(refer table F.V. below, 15years @ 6%)	2.3966
3. Future value of savings (1 x 2)	119,829
C. Calculating Monthly Savings Required:	
1. Anticipated shortfall (A.5 – B.3)	356,000
2. Future value factor for an annuity	21.5786
(refer F.V.A table, 15years @ 5%)	
3. Annual savings required (1÷ 2)	16,500
4. Monthly savings required (3 ÷ 12)	1,375

Here it is relevant to mention that your calculation is likely to be off the mark, and your education fund can be more or less than the required funds depending on whether you adapt a conservative or optimist approach respectively while selecting inflation rate and rate of return on investments. While it is important to be self-sufficient in the child's education planning, you should also explore how you can make the most of tax and other benefits, which differ from state to state as well as from time to time. And remember that maximizing savings and returns on your investments is always a good idea irrespective of the intended goals since investment goals are interchangeable.

The whole exercise encourages you and your family to be conscious of the importance of education goals, which have many other intangible benefits. If possible, you should involve the child and other family members in this endeavor since the whole exercise has many motivational and emotional benefits, which incidentally serve the core purpose of acquiring good education.

Future Value Factors (Table F.V.)

Periods	4%	6%	8%	10%
1	1.0400	1.0600	1.0800	1.1000
2	1.0816	1.1236	1.1664	1.2100
3	1.1249	1.1910	1.2597	1.3310
4	1.1699	1.2625	1.3605	1.4641
5	1.2167	1.3382	1.4693	1.6105
6	1.2653	1.4185	1.5869	1.7716
7	1.3159	1.5036	1.7138	1.9487
8	1.3686	1.5938	1.8509	2.1436
9	1.4233	1.6895	1.9990	2.3579
10	1.4802	1.7908	2.1589	2.5937
11	1.5395	1.8983	2.3316	2.8531
12	1.6010	2.0122	2.5182	3.1384
13	1.6651	2.1329	2.7196	3.4523
14	1.7317	2.2609	2.9372	3.7975
15	1.8009	2.3966	3.1722	4.1772
16	1.8730	2.5404	3.4259	4.5950
17	1.9479	2.6928	3.7000	5.0545
18	2.0258	2.8543	3.9960	5.5599
19	2.1068	3.0256	4.3157	6.1159
20	2.1911	3.2071	4.6610	6.7275

Future Value of Annuity Factors (Table F.V.A.)

Periods	3%	4%	5%	6%	7%
1	1.0000	1.0000	1.0000	1.0000	1.0000
2	2.0300	2.0400	2.0500	2.0600	2.0700
3	3.0909	3.1216	3.1525	3.1836	3.2149
4	4.1836	4.2465	4.3101	4.3746	4.4399
5	5.3091	5.4163	5.5256	5.6371	5.7507
6	6.4684	6.6330	6.8019	6.9753	7.1533
7	7.6625	7.8983	8.1420	8.3938	8.6540
8	8.8923	9.2142	9.5491	9.8975	10.2598
9	10.1591	10.5828	11.0266	11.4913	11.9780
10	11.4639	12.0061	12.5M9	13.1808	13.8164
11	12.8078	13.4864	14.2068	14.9716	15.7836
12	14.1920	15.0258	15.9171	16.8699	17.8885
13	15.6178	16.6268	17.7130	18.8821	20.1406
14	17.0863	18.2919	19.598	21.0151	22.5505
15	18.5989	20.0236	21.5786	23.2760	25.1290
16	20.1569	21.8245	23.6575	25.6725	27.8881
17	21.7616	23.6975	25.8404	28.2129	30.8402
18	23.4144	25.6454	28.1324	30.9057	33.9990
19	25.1169	27.6712	30.5390	33.7600	37.3790
20	26.8704	29.7781	33.0660	36.7856	40.9955

Though the scope of this book is limited to personal money matters, it is relevant to emphasize the importance of holistic planning to secure your child's future. While planning for your child's future, you need to have the bi-focal ability to see both the big picture and the financial aspects.

People often consider that children's future planning is just about arranging a corpus to meet expenses like education and wedding. Children's future planning is typically equated with planning finances for their future. Why holistic aspects are often subordinated to the financial aspects even by well-informed parents? Because we easily understand the language of money.

Most of us have materialistic tendencies, and consider money as a reliable yardstick. And wherever money is involved, there will be people willing to take advantage. When you google "children's future planning," you will get more than five million results. But almost all pertain to the financial aspects. In a world falling to pieces under the impact of a somewhat corrupt technological avalanche, it is so easy to use concern to get people to do what you want. While vested interests try to exploit parents' concern for their children, many conscientious parents maintain the right balance between financial and other factors to provide the holistic upbringing to their children.

Your child's future planning is not just about school and college expenses. There are other equally important factors such as right career planning and transforming the child into a well-grounded individual. The emphasis should be on the all round development of the child.

Parents have an integral role to play in shaping a child's overall personality. Molding the child into a responsible, productive and conscientious citizen is one of the big tasks for parents. They are privileged to have such a challenging responsibility to nurture the God's creations.

One of the most fulfilling experience of life is to witness the impact of your child's future planning unfold before your eyes and to see your child evolving into a well rounded human being who is a real asset to the society and humanity.

5.3 Creating Retirement Reserves

Retirement is a scary prospect for many people, especially when they think about the absence of monthly remuneration. With increasing lifespan, often retirement reserves comprising of both personal savings and retirement benefits are not enough for retirement, particularly when one is not sure about the post retirement period one has to brave out on these savings. People are realizing the need to be financially independent even after retirement, as they do not expect the government or others to bear the burden of their old age.

While adventuring to redefine retirement in my book Vision Revision, I have emphasized a great deal on the health and social consequences of retirement deliberately skipping the financial aspects. The objective was just to trigger a healthy discussion on the relatively inconspicuous but equally important themes, which are often overlooked while attending to the more glorified and commercial theme, namely, financial planning for retirement. We live in a world where financial aspects of retirement are enthroned, and health, professional and social aspects are often subordinated. In fact, people often consider retirement planning as just planning finances for retirement. The intention was not to undermine the importance of financial management but to reinforce it.

Moreover, our financial health and physical health are mutually dependent and both enhance our life, and quality of our life. There is no contradiction between the two. Each gives valuable support to the other. So we need to accord equal priority to the both, as we cannot enjoy money without health or health without money.

The subject of the book mandates me to address here only the financial concerns relating to the post retirement life. And I expect that after attending to the financial issues discussed in the earlier chapters, readers are likely to be in good shape to take care of their financial concerns of the golden years. Yet, the financial planning for retirement is not as simple and clear-cut exercise as often made out by the vested interests. It can be a very simple exercise but for numerous variables working waveringly. Many variables are external factors, i.e., factors beyond your control and hence cannot be accurately projected for future planning. Can you forecast rate of return on your investments after a decade? Can you predict fuel prices for the next year? Can you foresee health problems as well as related expenses after two decades? Can you foretell inflation rate for the next five years? Questions abound with no concrete solutions.

Just consider the consequences of price increases on your living expenses at various inflation rates. When inflation goes up, it does not mean returns on your market instruments will also go up. Returns on your market investments may possibly go down resulting in a double whack. Can you reasonably forecast your cost of living when you are 80 years old? The following table attempts to explore the impact of inflation on living expenses in percentage terms by considering inflation at 4% and 8%.

Consequences of Inflation on Retirees

Retirement Age	% Increase in cost of living by age 80	
Years	Inflation @ 4%	Inflation @ 8%
50	224	906
55	167	585
60	119	366
65	80	217

With just a few percentage points variation in one variable, i.e. inflation, your retirement budget may possibly go in for a toss.

You may wonder what is the use of a comprehensive plan when we cannot predict the basic factors correctly. Perhaps you are right. But then, we know the statistically proven fact that traveling is one of the biggest risk factors, yet we cannot and do not give up traveling. However, we strive to make our travels as risk-free as possible.

I do not want to depict a gloomy picture. What I am emphasizing is that it is an uncertain picture where one cannot be at ease by superficially balancing the retirement needs with the retirement reserves. I just intend to give a 360 degrees view of the retirement planning. This you may not get from your financial advisor, as s/he may perhaps like to skip some points that are counterproductive to her/his business interests. No wonder financial services are big business and are getting more and more profitable, often at the expense of gullible persons. However, one need not lose motivation because the doers can always find a way out, as we shall discuss shortly. Besides, in actuality, many negative and positive factors often counteract one another and the net negative impact, if any, is likely to be marginal. What is more, we tend to habituate ourselves to the present and blank out the distant time, which minimizes the psychological impact of negatives enabling us to harness the positives.

In view of the many indeterminate factors at play, financial planning for retirement may be a challenging task but its importance cannot be overlooked. Developing a financial plan is imperative to understand our preparedness for the sunset years. The golden years can be a time of enjoyment or the beginning of a nightmare depending on the adequacy of our financial preparedness for the post retirement period. A recent study by HSBC found that people who planned for retirement had five times the assets of those who did not. Our retirement plan provides us a framework that shows us the direction and the way forward to secure our financial future. The benefits of financial planning for later years outweigh the uncertainties and challenges of the process. Here we sum up some of the important advantages of financial planning for retirement.

- ✓ It provides a clear-cut blueprint of your finances during retirement and enables you to strike the right balance between savings and spending.

✓ It can relatively insulate you from the vagaries of inflation, market volatilities, dwindling returns, etc.

✓ It empowers you to take good care of yourself and your loved ones.

✓ Optimum planning ensures optimum use of resources, thereby enabling you to bequeath a decent estate to your kith and kin.

✓ It attempts to make your golden years rather dull by taking away financial suspicions, surprises and suspense.

✓ Financial planning process not just makes you financially independent but also makes you aware that you are independent. And that makes the difference.

Accumulation and Expending Stages

Financial planning for retirement can be categorized into accumulation and expending stages. First stage is pre retirement phase when we save for retirement, and the second stage is post retirement phase when we require a regular income. The financial planning process for retirement essentially aims to manage the factors influencing accumulation and expending stages. It attempts not merely to counterbalance these two phases but also to create a reasonable surplus for contingences of the post retirement phase.

Many people have a propensity to balance accumulation and expending phases theoretically with reference to the prevailing indicators. They are usually more prone to go by the current estimates of many unpredictable factors such as life expectancy, inflation and interest rates. These apparently apt estimates cannot be too reliable to guarantee our financial security in the far-away future. So here, merely balancing savings with the projected expenses may not be an infallible strategy.

To work out a reliable strategy, we can take a cue from this famous saying of Archimedes, "Give me a long enough lever and I can lift the earth." What he meant was that if he could stand far enough away from the earth he could use a lever to move the earth. His point was that we could lift anything with a long enough lever by shifting the fulcrum to the right position. We can apply this simple yet foolproof concept to plan our finances for retirement. Here our lever is our indefinite lifespan and the fulcrum is the retirement age. We simply need to shift the fulcrum to the right to expand the left side of the lever, i.e., the accumulation phase that can provide more than sufficient leverage to take care of the financial concerns of the post retirement life. The following diagram distinctly depicts the rewards of stretching the known and executable accumulation phase to adequately provide for the relatively unknown and dubious post retirement phase. Here we are shifting only the retirement age, assuming all other variables like savings amount and interest rate at the same level.

Retirement Reserves – Standard Retirement Age

30   << Age Years >>   90
                             60

Accumulation Phase   Expending Phase

Retirement Reserves – Extended Retirement Age

30   << Age Years >>   90
                             70

Accumulation Phase   Expending Phase

In the second case, accumulation phase can potentially boost retirement reserves to more than double as compared to the first case. The concept of time value of money plays a part in providing more than proportionate advantage in the second case. In addition, the duration of expending phase is much less in the second case.

We know that the retirement planning process looks at many variable factors such as age when you start saving, savings amount, return on investments, retirement age, expenses during retirement, inflation and market dynamics. The planning process is also influenced by many personal factors, like family responsibilities, health concerns, personal goals, preferred lifestyle and the rest. But the two factors, viz. Present age when you start saving for retirement and Retirement age, can really make a big difference to your accumulation endeavors, as you will find hereunder.

Early Saver Advantage

In the process of financial planning for retirement, the most important point to keep in mind is the power of compounding. This can do wonders to your retirement corpus if you have a long way to go before you retire. The benefits of starting early to secure your financial future cannot be overemphasized. This is the best antidote to meet the challenges of longer life span and dwindling returns on the financial investments. It gives you a good head start owing to the time value of money in conjunction with the long duration.

You may be surprised to note that if you start saving at the age of 20 and at the interest rate of 20% per annum, you need to save less than $2 per month to retire at the age of seventy with one million dollars. Employed people invariably appreciate the benefits of long-term saving. They exercise thrift and start saving early in career to ensure that retirement does not become a financial nightmare. In fact, they work out retirement needs early in career and save accordingly for the retirement. The following table quantifies the benefits of starting early to save for your retirement. It shows the amount you need to save every month to accumulate a million dollars by the time of retirement. The first column shows the years you need to save and the second, third, and fourth columns give the amount you need to save every month to amass one million dollars at the interest rate of 5%, 10%, or 15% respectively.

Monthly Savings Required to Accumulate One Million

Saving period	Saving every month at the interest rate ($)		
(Years)	5%	10%	15%
5	15081	13650	12360
10	6625	5229	4104
15	3862	2623	1751
20	2520	1455	813
25	1746	847	392
30	1254	507	192
40	690	188	47
50	398	72	12

Extending Career

The structure of this chapter mandates me to discuss pure money matters influencing retirement finances. Yet unable to restrain myself, I reiterate that the best strategy is to continue to work beyond the traditional retirement age to derive optimum health and financial benefits. This way you can extend the accumulation phase, which not only increases the savings but also shrinks the distribution phase as well as the financial needs during retirement. Even if you have missed on the early saver advantage, this provides you a chance to make up for the lost opportunity. We try to elaborate this with the help of a hypothetical example.

For the sake of simplicity, let us assume that a person aspires to provide for 30 years in retirement after working for 30 years. He plans to provide for his inflation-adjusted retirement expenses from pension and other resources. But he anticipates that his retirement income deficiency will be practically $100,000 per annum, which he wants to balance out with an annuity. With a view to meet this shortfall, he intends to save $1,000 per month @

8% from age 35 until age 60 when he will retire (column A). But then, his planner works out that he needs $1.13 million at the time of retirement to buy an annuity of $100,000 per annum @ 8% for 30 years whereas his savings will accumulate to only $0.88 million. He will face a deficit of $0.25 million at the time of retirement.

Retirement Funds Worksheet

Particulars	Standard Retirement A	Early Saver B	Extended Career C	Early + Extended D
Accumulation Phase:				
Savings Started at Age:-	35	30	35	30
Retirement Age:-	60	60	70	70
Savings Period- years	25	30	35	40
Annual Savings	12000	12000	12000	12000
1. Retirement Funds @ 8% = million $	0.88	1.36	2.07	3.11
Distribution Phase:				
Retirement Period- years (up to 90 years)	30	30	20	20
Annuity/Retire-ment Needs (Amount $ p.a.)	100000	100000	100000	100000
2. Sum Payable for Annuity @ 8% = million $	1.13	1.13	0.98	0.98
(1 – 2) Surplus for inheritance = million $	-0.25	0.23	1.09	2.13

Let us take the case B wherein he opts to avail early saver advantage and intends to save from age 30 instead of age 35. In this case, his retirement savings will increase to $1.36 million that is sufficient to meet the requirement of $1.13 million at the time of retirement.

Next alternative is the case C wherein he prefers to extend his career by another 10 years after the scheduled retirement date. Here he will save for 35 years and spend 20 years in retirement. In this case, his retirement kitty will swell to $2.07 million as against the requirement of $0.98 million at the time of retirement. He will have a surplus of $1.09 million at the time of retirement, which he can earmark for his loved ones.

Now take the case D in which he intends to take early saver advantage as well as extended career benefits. Here his retirement capital will add up to $3.11 million that is more than three times his retirement needs. Retirement funds worksheet on the previous page clearly illustrates these examples.

As is clear from the above, starting early and extending career can give you an incredible financial advantage to make your golden years truly golden. You should analyze your own accumulation and expending stages by incorporating your estimates in the above table. You can refer online calculators or tables for 'future value of annuity' and 'present value of annuity' to compute retirement corpus and sum payable for annuity respectively. In case of any clarification or for getting your personal worksheet of accumulation and expending stages, you should contact your financial advisor or drop us a line. After appreciating the impact of early saving and extended career on retirement funds, we take up the essential steps involved in the process of fortifying your financial future.

Steps in Financial Planning for Retirement

People are living longer than before. Yet, a few are still not preparing themselves to sufficiently provide for extra golden years. Some people are closing the eyes to the changed circumstances by clinging to the outdated notions, which were pertinent when retirement period and financial needs were significantly less.

However, more and more people are realizing the need to be financially independent throughout their life. With financial independence and increase in the disposable income, senior people can opt for an independent life and carve an impressive identity of their own in retirement. Optimal financial planning let them live a life of their own, enjoying their space and sense of dignity. Most people appreciate the importance of retirement planning and often brood over it, albeit in an unstructured manner. Many are now realizing the need to establish a definite plan for an honorable subsistence during the later years as they do not expect state and others to bear the burden of their second childhood. Even in the developed countries, the responsibility of financial planning for retirement is shifting away from the state and towards the individual citizen. With an eye to ensure financial security during retirement, we discuss here below five important steps in the process of retirement planning.

Envisioning Retirement

Before you can effectively develop a financial plan for your postretirement years, you need to figure out what is your definition of golden retirement. Understanding your motivations for the contented post retirement life will better prepare you to achieve your goals. Then you can wisely proceed to quantify cost implications of your desired life style in retirement.

At this stage, you ought to envision your desired lifestyle in retirement. You have to be well aware of your own definition of a comfortable retired life that will make you and your family happy during your golden years. In essence, you have to create a vision of your perfect retirement and determine what your version of happiness will cost. Next, you need to explore how you can organize your finances in order to pay for that happiness. This will facilitate you to review your financial needs during retirement as well as stimulate your thinking on how to realign your capital along the lines of your retirement vision.

Reviewing Personal Financial Status

Periodically you are supposed to review your personal financial status, as a routine part of your money management regimen. Here it entails revisiting your financial status from the sole perspective of retirement planning to ensure financial security during retirement.

Your retirement vision will enable you to prioritize various components of your personal financial status in proportion to your retirement needs and desires. At various stages in your life, your needs vary thereby prompting you to accord different priorities to the various components of your capital. In the early stages of career, one can afford to be aggressive in investments, which incidentally suits well at that stage to fulfill the long-term retirement objectives. But one has to gradually shift the gears on the way to retirement. One should adopt a neutral approach during middle age that will eventually give way to a more conservative approach in the last stage of work life. The idea is to invest retirement finances in such a way that balance gradually shifts towards fixed return investments over a period of time. This typical pattern has become the hallmark of retirement planning because it creates an optimal balance between wealth creation and retirement objectives. The following table illustrates a basic assets prioritization model at various life stages.

Retirement Reserves— Assets Prioritization Model

Age/Priority → ↓Assets	30's	40's	50's	60's
House	Medium	High	High	High
Equity	High	High	Medium	Low
Fixed return	Low	Medium	Medium	High
Life insurance	Medium	Medium	High	Medium
Health insurance	Low	Medium	High	High
Annuity	Low	Medium	Medium	High

The above-mentioned general indicators are changeable depending on the various personal factors. These priorities just give a broad idea as to how financial status should move forward while traversing different stages of life cycle.

As it happens, your priorities will be influenced by your unique set of circumstances, such as financial status, family members and their priorities, adequacy of retirement nest egg, your obligations, probable inheritance, need and desire to bequeath, and the rest.

Priorities always differ from person to person, but one factor, i.e., house is on top of the agenda of most people. This shows the commitment of working class towards their retirement vision as the house is invariably the primary factor in the retirement planning process.

Estimating Expenses

In order to prepare adequately for your retirement years, you should know or at least have an inkling of your monthly expenses. You need to estimate your retirement expenses based on your preferred standard of living and other relevant factors in order to find out what your version of happiness will cost. Experts suggest that you will require 70 to 80 percent of your current expenses after retirement to maintain your lifestyle. This may well be deceptively true in the short term. It cannot be taken for granted, as you cannot precisely forecast many variables, such as inflation rate, future requirements, family obligations, and healthcare expenses.

In spite of all this, it would help you if you quantify your retirement expenses based on the type of lifestyle you plan to have and the timing of your retirement. The process to identify your retirement needs and desires will make you sentient of your preparedness and guide you to organize your accumulation part accordingly. Remember, some animals and careless people do not prepare for their later years, but wise people plan for the future and enjoy their golden years.

Here is a table exemplifying the process of estimating monthly expenses.

Forecasting Retirement Expenses

Monthly Expenses	Amount	Likely Change +/- %	% of Total
Living Expenses			25-35
Personal Debt Expenses			5-10
Housing Expenses			10-25
Health & Family Care			15-35
Transport Expenses			5-10
Recreational Expenses			3-10
Miscellaneous Expenses			5-15
Total Expenses			

The above analysis will help you determine the probable status of your expenses during the retirement years. This will give you a reasonable idea of your expense replacement ratio that is the percentage of your pre-retirement expenses replaced during retirement.

Retirement professionals recommend a range from 60 to 80% for this ratio for the majority of employed people. Generally, the lower monthly income entails a higher ratio and vice versa. You need to calculate your applicable ratio to forecast your expenses for the future period. In addition, you should set aside an additional amount for miscellaneous expenses that cannot be planned.

The impact of inflation on your expenses is a serious issue as it can lower the purchasing power of your defined income. You need to calculate your expenses during retirement with realistic inflation in mind. You can use online calculators or inflation charts to estimate your total expenses.

Impact of Inflation on Expenses in Retirement

Year	Total Expenses @ 4% inflation	Total Expenses @ 8% inflation
2020		
2021		
2023		
2024		
...		
....		
2030		
...		
.....		
2050		

While it is usually better to seek a professional's help with retirement reckonings, your active involvement is indispensable whatever the case may be. You need to keep in mind that no one can precisely estimate your future expenses without considering a broad spectrum of your personal issues. Your personal view of retirement life-style and the associated expenses along with inflation estimates will have a lot to do with guesstimating your future expenses more accurately.

Estimating Income

Once you have determined your retirement expenses, the next step is to examine your retirement income situation. It is a simple process of ascertaining your cash inflows during retirement in order to examine the sufficiency and sustainability of these during your lifetime. It cautions you in time by recognizing the gap between reality and your retirement vision when your future cash inflows are not in sync with your expense projections.

In order to carry out this step logically, it should be organized into three parts:

> Quantifying External Sources of Income
> Working out Income Deficiency
> Examining Personal Sources

Quantifying External Sources of Income

We can broadly classify the sources of retirement income as external and personal. The external sources primarily consist of employers' pension and state benefits. The external sources of income vary significantly from case to case depending on the employers' policies and applicable state benefits, yet they are more or less defined for an individual. Even though these benefits are a function of several factors, such as retirement age, status, self-contributions and the like, they can be considered as stable in nature for an individual because these are typically nonarbitrary. An individual may not have much control over these since the external authorities govern these, but s/he must fully understand these to take maximum advantage of these benefits. In view of the predetermined character of the external sources of income and adequate awareness of these among beneficiaries, they do not deserve further discussion. Nevertheless, it is important to determine these correctly in order to quantify retirement income deficiency to meet the estimated expenses.

Working out Income Deficiency

Retirement income deficiency is simply the difference between the defined external sources of income and the estimated expenses during retirement. Most employed people do not experience significant income deficiency because they are innately thrifty with money. They are used to live a simple and responsible life. And they inculcate the same values in their children, who are generally self-supporting at the time of their retirement. More often than not, they fulfill most of their responsibilities by the time they retire. But in a few cases, the income deficiency is likely to be considerable. Whether this is owing to the deficient external sources of income or due to the higher anticipated expenses, they have to bridge the gap on their own from their personal resources. Now we discuss how one should use the personal sources to offset the income deficit.

Examining Personal Sources

There are two common methods to make up the income deficiency from the personal resources– the capital preservation method and the capital utilization method. Unique circumstances of an individual will determine whether one should go for any one of the methods or an appropriate combination of the two. The need and desire to bequeath assets to the kith and kin favors the preservation method whereas retirement needs may perhaps press for the capital utilization method. However, one needs to strike a balance between the two considering all the pertinent personal factors.

When you opt for the capital preservation method to meet the shortfall in income, you have to depend on the returns from your investments. This method necessitates a substantial capital base at the time of retirement. You should make an estimate of the future value of your investments and other assets at the scheduled time of retirement. This will give an indication of sufficiency or otherwise of your retirement corpus to generate adequate income. Here are some common sources of income.

- ✓ Interest returns on fixed income instruments
- ✓ Dividends on equity holdings
- ✓ Rental income from real estate
- ✓ Trading/Arbitrage income from investments
- ✓ Income from securities lending
- ✓ Profit from writing 'out of money' call/put options on self holdings

The capital utilization method notionally reckons that all the assets will be liquidated to meet the income deficiency during retirement. However, people usually adopt a gradual and staggered approach even if they decide to liquidate all the assets for their retirement needs. Some of the options preferred by the common people are discussed hereafter.

Cashing investments: One can make up the shortfall in retirement income by gradually selling investments. One needs to update the personal financial status in order to make a viable and cost efficient plan to liquidate investments. Depending on the personal financial status, i.e., the type and nature of assets, an advantageous strategy can be worked out to maximize the cash inflows besides ensuring the continuity of the income. One may consider converting investments including the cash value of life insurance to cash and opt for fixed return instruments or an annuity to ensure steady cash inflows. One has to keep in mind several factors, such as age, health situation, net assets, family situation, and so on to devise a suitable and lasting strategy.

Annuities: An annuity is a flexible financial instrument that allows accumulating retirement savings and then reaping the benefits of savings in the form of periodic payments or a lump sum payment. Dictionary meaning of annuity is a fixed sum of money paid each year. But, in practice, it refers to periodical payments, generally monthly. It is an excellent tool to ensure lifelong cash inflows to take care of essential needs.

Annuity and pension are similar as both provide regular payments to retired people either by the state, employer, or from an investment fund. The need for annuity is quite different from that of life insurance. Yet both life insurance and annuity are protective measures. As insurance safeguards a person from the uncertainties of early death, life annuities safeguard a person against the risk of exhausting capital if s/he lives too long. It is an instrument of choice for such people who are not so good at managing their money. Annuities offer much flexibility to retirees who can choose the one that suits their situation from numerous options. There are various types of annuities, e.g. fixed and variable, single life or joint life, single premium or periodic premium, refund feature or no refund, and so on.

Reverse Mortgage: People who do not have many investments but own a house can opt for reverse mortgage to cope with the retirement income shortfall. We are well conversant with the concept of mortgage or home loan. Reverse mortgage, as the name suggests, is a reversal of the mortgage concept. It is aimed to help senior retirees who are 'house rich', but 'cash poor'. Retirees are not generally eligible for loans, but they can borrow big bucks-either lump sum or as periodic payments against their house.

The borrowers can live in their house as well as receive cash installments to meet the income deficiency for the rest of their life. The spouse can also avail the benefits as a co-borrower, even after the demise of borrower. Moreover, the borrower is not required to repay the loan, which is repaid through the sale of the house on the borrower's death. The borrowers usually have the option to prepay the loan with interest at any time during the loan tenor. The borrower's heirs can also repay the loan amount with interest and have the mortgage released.

Other sources: To augment the retirement income, one can also explore other options, such as increasing the rate of return within the acceptable risk parameters, extending the retirement age, cutting down the retirement expenses, adapting some lifestyle changes, seeking help from family or friends, and so on. If time and other factors permit, one should first consider adding to the savings for the retirement period. Though these are strictly personal choices, one may like to weigh the impact as well as the pros and cons of each supplemental income source on the retirement income shortfall before seriously considering these in the retirement reckonings.

Managing the Plan

Investors who are flush with funds can afford to take this exercise flippantly. But all are not so fortunate. In many cases, state and employer benefits are not adequate to meet even the necessities. This problem is further compounded by the inflation, which may diminish the purchasing power of fixed pension and/or annuities as well as the nest egg earmarked for the retirement. Duration of retirement is slowly but surely extending and as such, people are spending more time in retirement. It is expected to go beyond one-third of our life. All these factors necessitate a planned approach to the retirement issues. To get a clear-cut picture of retirement planning, you can now outline your plan broadly in the following format. Understanding the above steps will help you to complete this exercise in a rational manner.

Financial Specifics of Retirement

Particulars	2011-$\Rightarrow$	2021-$\Rightarrow$	2031-$\Rightarrow$
A. Essence of Retirement Vision			
B. Personal Financial Status: - ... - -			
C. Estimated Expenses: - ... - - -....			
D. Income Sources: D.1 External sources- - ... -.... D.2 Personal sources- - ... -....			
E. Retirement Income (D.1-C) Surplus+/Deficit-			

While managing your plan, you need to focus on the two aspects— how your numbers stack up for the first year in retirement and how the numbers are likely to fluctuate going forward. These two aspects will give you the sixth sense to take the timely corrective measures to avert the probable problems in retirement. Managing your retirement plan is not just about ensuring your retirement income needs; it also offers you a chance to capitalize on market opportunities.

After setting up your retirement plan aimed at making your golden years truly golden, you need to work assiduously towards achieving your retirement objectives. And you should be very clear about the distinction between 'what you need' and 'what you want' to get the most from your planning exercise. Periodically, you should also monitor your financial plan to make sure it is on the right track. But you have to follow a somewhat flexible approach while reviewing or revising your plan in the light of latest developments. Remember, a course correction because of minor issues is not always a good idea. Many a times things fall into place as time passes. So be cautiously optimistic while evaluating your progress.

In the ultimate analysis of financial independence, what is really important is that you could do what truly matters to you even while covering the last lap of your life's journey.

5.4 Fortifying Family's Financial Future

The underlying objective of the financial vision process is to optimize the financial well-being of your family. All elements of the financial vision process aim at securing your family's future, particularly the financial needs and wants. You are a senior and responsible member of your family. The financial vision process expects you to officiate as a Chief Financial Officer of your family and take good care of your family members. And while you are in the driver's seat, it also expects you to protect your family from any unforeseen event that may be a burden to your family in the future.

Your role as a practical and empathetic CFO requires you to not just bring home the bacon, but also provide for all contingencies in a realistic manner so as to ensure that your family's present and future needs are assured even if you are not there to care for them. The structure of the financial vision process makes this painful yet inevitable transition somewhat less painful for the family members due to the carefully planned procedural and protective elements discussed in the chapter "Financial Vision Process: An Overview." These elements are designed to enable other family members to assume your responsibilities when the situation demands it. But you are responsible to put in place all the procedural and protective elements.

You do not have to make the most money to be considered a great success. When it comes to success and happiness, your family's well being is the most important yardstick. It is the most relevant and real criterion of success. Family life brings along many joys and pleasures to life, but there also some responsibilities. Securing your family's future is one of them. In fact, it is your prime responsibility.

But then, you are unique, just like everyone else. You are not a robot; you cannot be replaced. If something should go wrong, you want to be assured that your family can continue to live in a reasonable fashion. Your family's financial future is too important to leave to chance. Your family's well being is the reason why you work hard all your life. And you would certainly like to ensure that your family members continue to enjoy the kind of life that you want them to have.

So, you must make sure that at least one family member is aware of your financial state of affairs. It is important that a dependable family member is familiar with all your documents and financial matters, particularly procedural and protective elements. If you are not in a position to involve any family member in your financial matters, reinforce your proxy file system discussed in the chapter "Getting Organized." Your proxy system will serve as a back up arrangement when you are not around. This is intended to help someone from your family to take charge when you are no more or when you are unable to handle the financial issues due to disability or old age. Remember, your financial records follow a simple, structured approach, which makes it easy for any layperson to understand your financial documents.

People do not like to think about what happens when they die. But if they do not, their families could suffer. Securing your family's financial future is not difficult if you are open and serious about it. Whether it is very easy or not, primarily depends on how well you have understood and followed the financial vision process. However, a few factors need emphasis to further fortify your family's financial future. Here we again take up the life insurance and estate planning from the perspective of what is best for the family.

Life Insurance

The life is not insurable. However, there are many potentially serious outcomes that can be insured against. Life insurance is meant to protect the family against the financial impact of losing the major breadwinner or the homemaker. We often overlook the role of homemaker because here no money exchanges hands. We conveniently forget the earning potential of the homemaker until we have to pay for the childcare and all the other duties carried out around the home.

Anyone who expects that there could be expenses after they die should have life insurance. It is particularly important if you have a dependent spouse and/or children. Life insurance is one of the most important purchases you can make to ensure that your family members will be taken care of if something unforeseen should happen to you. Life insurance is a necessity because it is the safety net for your loved ones. Remember, your family's security comes first. There is nothing more important than your family's future.

While considering your life insurance needs, it is a good idea to step back from the sales pitches and be sure that you are only considering your family's needs before you make a purchase decision. As you analyze your insurance needs, bear in mind that life insurance is not for you; it is for your survivors. You need life insurance when you have family members who count on your income.

Before you purchase life insurance, you should have a clear understanding of two basic questions:

» How much insurance do you need?
» What type of Insurance suits you?

Life insurance needs analysis

The following worksheet is designed to assist you in calculating how much life insurance is needed for your survivors considering that your family will maintain the same standard of living. This worksheet provides a framework that will help you estimate your insurance needs. Keep in mind that the life insurance needs analysis worksheet assumes that capital deployed in the available financial assets can offset your life insurance needs.

And remember, in the case of life insurance, individual needs vary with circumstances. Just like everything else, it changes over time and as such, you should review your insurance needs every 2- 3 years or whenever your family circumstances change. You should periodically ensure that your insurance policies still meet your insurance needs for your current situation.

Life Insurance Needs Analysis Worksheet

Part I	Capital Required:-	Amount
A.	A. Final Expenses:	
A..1	Funeral, legal, estate costs, etc.	
B	Debt Liquidation:	
B.1	Mortgage balance	
B.2	Outstanding Car loans	
B.3	Credit card balances	
B.4	Other loan balances	
C.	Special Needs:	
C.1	Children education	
C.2	Spouse training/education	
C.3	Other known needs	
D.	Other Financial Needs:	
E.	Income Needs:	
E.1	Annual living expenses	
E.2	*Less* income available	
E.3	Total income needs	
	{(E.1-E.2) x factor for no. of years }	
	(for factor refer point 6 below)	
I	Total Capital Required (total A to E)	
Part II	Capital Available:-	
F.	Current Life Insurance Cover	
G.	Savings and Investments:	
G.1	Financial Investments	
G.2	Other Available investments	
H.	Other Resources:	
H.1	Other assets & resources	
II	Total Capital Available (total F to H)	
III	Life Insurance Needed	
	I –II= capital required - capital available	

1. Final expenses (A) can be estimated as percentage of net assets or an approximate lump-sum figure.
2. You should consider only outstanding loan amount, i.e., principal amount payable for debt liquidation (B.1 to B.4).
3. For special needs like child education, actual calculations done earlier should be taken. You can take present value of future

education expenses with adjustments for the difference in the inflation on education costs and returns on investments.

4. Annual living expenses (E.1) are usually between 60%- 75% of previous total income. However, consider any lifestyle changes. To arrive at this figure, you may refer income statement and monthly budget prepared earlier.

5. Income available (E.2) is the annual income your family would receive from other sources, e.g., spouse's income, fixed pension and other benefits. But do not consider returns on assets because assets are taken in part II of this worksheet.

6. To arrive at the total income needs (E.3), multiply the income deficit (i.e., income to be replaced) by the appropriate factor: 10 years x 8.1; 15 years x 11.1; 20 years x 13.6; 25 years x 15.6; 30 years x 17.3; 35 years x 18.7 and 40 years x 20.0.

7. Financial investments (G.1) cover bank accounts, fixed return accounts, stocks, bonds, mutual funds, etc. Refer your personal financial status to fill up the capital available figures.

If you end up with a very high figure that is beyond your budget for insurance premium, you should go through the analysis again and try to find any mistakes as well as other areas where you can compromise. If necessary, you should make a new worksheet only with the crucial elements in the part I and start making adjustments from that. Alternatively, to assess your situation rationally, you can use the following formula where 'Total amount at stake' is the capital required in the above worksheet, and 'Total wealth' can be taken from your personal financial status. A higher ratio indicates a higher need for life insurance and vice versa.

Relative value of the risk= Total amount at stake ÷ Total wealth

What type of Insurance suits you?

Once you have determined how much insurance cover you need, you need to find the right kind of policy that serves your purpose. There are various types of policies available in the market. But with an eye to securing the family's financial future, we need to explore two basic types of life insurance: term insurance and whole life insurance.

Term insurance is a low-cost, high-value insurance cover where one is insured only against the risk of death. A term life insurance policy covers you for a specific number of years, or term, such as 5, 10, or 30 years. It is meant as a temporary form of protection. It pays a death benefit only if you die in the insured term. Premium rates are based on the probability of death, so as you age, premium rates become higher. The cost of a term policy depends on the health of the insured, the length of the policy term, and the size of the benefit involved. A term life policy is a pure life insurance policy; it does not accrue any cash value. Once the policy term date is reached, you may renew your policy at a new rate, or forfeit your policy. These policies are less expensive, but when the policy's term is up, the policyholder's beneficiaries have no claim on a death benefit.

Whole life insurance policy has no specified term and provides guaranteed coverage until death. As long as your premiums are paid, you can live and reside anywhere in the world with no restrictions. Your premium rate remains the same throughout the entire life of the policy, making it less expensive over the life of the policy as far as insurance part is concerned. Moreover, a whole life policy accrues cash value. It provides coverage for your family while it simultaneously builds savings that you can use in many ways. The cash value that a whole life policy accrues can either be accessed by taking a loan against the cash value, or by surrendering the policy and cashing out. Whole life insurance is more expensive than term insurance since you pay the premium not only for insurance but also for the investment component.

You need to choose your life insurance policy based on your family's needs, your assets, and the affordability of the policy. Remember, every individual is different and his/her circumstances and protection needs are different, and one set of rules for insurance cannot be applied to all. That is why you have to make a rational decision yourself.

Estate Planning

Estate planning is the process of planning and arranging your succession and financial affairs. We have already discussed that estate planning requires you to draw on your discretion in respect of three main areas, viz. people planning, assets planning and transfer planning. Here we illustrate a basic estate-planning worksheet, which can help you to plan and organize your inheritance efficiently.

Sample Estate Planning Worksheet

Part I. Personal Information Part
- Your immediate family's information - names, dates of birth, contact details, and citizenship status, etc.
- Information of your parents, grandchildren, ex spouses and any other entity or person who is intended as a beneficiary.
- Names, addresses and contact details of people you want to serve as executors, trustees and guardians for your children.
- Names and contact details of power of attorney and health care decision maker.
- Any other information you may consider relevant.

Part II. Estate Analysis Part

Particulars	In Husband's Name $	In Wife's Name $	In Joint Names $
Details of Assets:			
Total Assets			
Details of Liabilities:			
Total Liabilities			
Life Insurance Details:			

Part III. Distribution Part

> Upon my passing, I would like my estate to pass as follows:
> ...

> I leave the rest, residue and remainder of my estate to my great-grandchildren as follows:
> ...

Estate planning is one of the most important things you can do for your family and your piece of mind. One of the greatest gifts you can leave your survivors is an organized estate.

Estate planning helps you manage your assets while you are alive and protects your family for the future. It entails arranging your affairs efficiently in order to maximize the value of your estate and minimize the expenses and taxes. Here we discuss some of the basic components of an estate plan

Will

A will is a legal declaration of how a person wishes his or her assets to be distributed after death. It is the central component of every estate plan. A will is also known as a last will and testament. A will is also used to determine guardianship of minor children and to set up trusts for heirs who may not have adequate knowledge of how to manage inherited assets. A person making a will is known in law as the `testator' (male) or 'testatrix' (female).

Although making a will is not mandatory by law, it is the best way to make sure your assets are passed on to your heirs exactly as you wish. If you die without a will, your property may be distributed according to the law rather than your wishes. Making a will is a sign of a responsible individual who plans ahead and cares for his family. It is never too early to make a will, but it can unfortunately be too late.

Wills are not just for the rich. It is important for you to make a will regardless of how much or how little money you have. There are many good reasons to make a will. Here are some important ones that may encourage the uninitiated ones to take it seriously.

- A will that clearly states your wishes is the best possible way to ensure that after death your estate will be dealt with according to your wishes.
- You choose who will carry out your wishes. You decide who is going to administer your estate. Executors and Trustees of choice can be appointed to deal with the administration of your estate. In the absence of a will, someone who you do not trust may wind up your estate.
- It helps to anticipate and avoid potential disputes between family members after your death. A will is the easiest way

to ensure that deserving people get your legacy. It goes a long way in ensuring that everyone gets what you wanted to give him or her and avoid unnecessary arguments amongst family members, which can arise when a deceased person's wishes are unclear.

- If there is no will, your estate may have to pay more tax unnecessarily, leaving less for your heirs. When you consider tax planning as an essential part of making a will, you can mitigate a potential inheritance tax liability.
- You can appoint guardian of your choice to ensure that the care of minor children passes to the right individual. You can also indicate in your will who you would like to provide the financial support to your under-age children.
- You can make individual gifts of cash or other assets to your chosen individuals or charities.
- Making a will is common sense and is probably less expensive than you might imagine. Cost of making a will is negligible but it could reap immeasurable benefits for your heirs.
- It is comforting to know that if something were to happen to you, you would have taken steps to ensure that your dependents faces the least amount of discomfort or financial crunch. Your will enables you to live the rest of your life without worrying about the future.

There is no good reason not to write a will. And it is always better to consult a professional to make your will and get it registered. But if your estate is small and easy to divide, you can always write your will yourself. Writing a will is easy when you first make a list of all beneficiaries and all your moveable and immoveable properties. A will should generally meet the following requirements.

- It must be in writing
- You must be over 18 when you make it
- You must have sufficient mental capacity to create the will and understand the effect it will have
- It must be signed and witnessed
- You must not have made it because of pressure from someone else.

When writing a will, you must first state your testamentary intent, such as 'This is my will.' The beginning of the will should also state that this will revokes all others. If you have an earlier will, it should be destroyed. A will generally includes a list of your assets, the names of all heirs, the proportion in which they will inherit your assets, the name of an executor who executes your will after your death, and names & signatures of two witnesses. However, you can customize your will for your specific needs. Customarily, the contents of a will consist of the following five components:

- First part deals with final expenses, i.e., how your final bills will be paid;
- Second part deals with estate liabilities, i.e., how the estate expenses and/or inheritance taxes will be paid;
- Third part deals with allocation of responsibilities, i.e., who will be in charge of overseeing the settling of your estate (the Executor or Executrix) and, if you have minor children, who will be responsible for raising the children (the Guardian);
- Fourth part deals with legacies, i.e., who will get what from your estate; and
- Fifth part deals with who will get the balance, if any, of your estate.

When writing your will, you should avoid ambiguity and precatory language, which is expressing a wish, since wishes have no legal effect. After writing your last will and testament, make sure you keep it in a safe place and the executor knows where it is located. Remember, preparing a will is not a one off event. You should review and revise your will on a regular basis, especially whenever there is a change in the circumstances that were at play when you initially prepared it.

Probate

Probate is a legal process whereby a court oversees the distribution of assets left by a deceased person's will. It typically involves filing a deceased person's will with the court, taking an inventory of the deceased's assets, paying all legal debts, and finally distributing the remaining assets to the beneficiaries. In some cases, this process can be time-consuming and tedious. Usually, the probate process is simplified for estates below a certain amount, but that amount varies according to the local law.

In the probate process, the executor of the will approaches the appropriate court in the county of the decedent's legal residence with the will on behalf of the decedent. When no will has been left, and thus no executor named by the decedent, then the spouse or a family member of the deceased can ask for a court-appointed administrator to settle debts and bequeath assets. Court-appointed administrators and executors have almost identical responsibilities and rights.

In order to avoid challenges during the probate process, a will must be clear, specific and legally valid. The will should make it absolutely clear how you want your assets and property to be distributed after you die. In case of any doubt, it is a good idea to have your will checked by a lawyer.

Living Will

Living will is a legal document that can speak for a patient who is unable to communicate. It is the first step to ensure that the patient is well prepared to face any kind of medical emergency when she or he is unable to make decisions. A living will may indicate specific care or treatment the person does or does not want performed under specific circumstances. It serves a crucial role in the health care planning.

The living will is the oldest form of advance directive. Advance directives are written instructions that tell your doctors what kind of treatment you will want if you become incapable to take your medical decisions. A living will does not give you the opportunity to select someone to make decisions for you, but allows you to specify the kind of treatment you want in specific situations. A living will is not to be confused with a last will and testament that distributes assets after a person's death.

Trusts

A trust is a legal entity that holds some assets for the benefit of another person or class of persons called the 'beneficiaries'. The person who creates the trust is called a grantor, donor, founder, or settlor. Grantor appoints a person or entity as trustee to manage the trust. The grantor also chooses the beneficiaries who will benefit from the trust. In some situations, the grantor can also act as trustee and beneficiary. But he needs to appoint a successor trustee and beneficiary in case he or she dies or becomes incapacitated.

A trust is a useful estate-planning tool since it does not go through the tedious and often protracted probate process. The following diagram depicts the relationship of the various entities in a trust.

The Basic Structure of a Trust

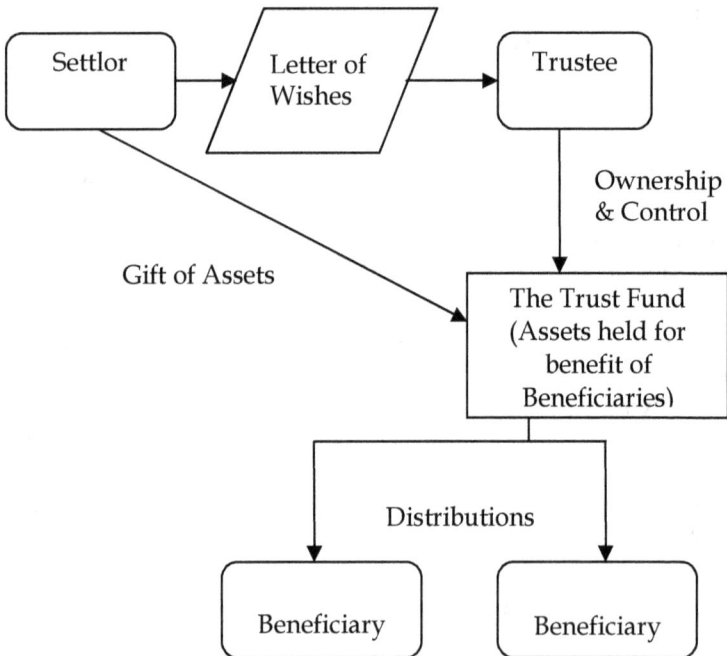

Most people believe that trusts are only for the wealthy and are too costly. Nothing could be further from the truth. Many families can take advantage of trusts in their estate planning. There are many different types of trusts that can be used to accomplish various estate planning goals and objectives. Trusts can be suitable for people with minor children or those who want to avoid having their estate go through the probate process after they die. Many people create trusts to preserve control and pass on their assets to their beneficiaries in an efficient and discreet manner. Here are some common benefits and objectives of using trusts in the estate planning process.

- To provide funds for children, dependents, etc.
- To reduce estate taxes and provide liquid assets to pay taxes and other expenses
- To protect assets and ensure methodical succession planning
- To avoid the expense and delay of probate
- To facilitate gifting to charities and institutions
- To facilitate management of finances and assets when you are out of action
- Privacy makes a trust an attractive option since the terms of a trust are not public while the terms of a will are public.

A trust provides a very flexible and efficient arrangement to meet the anticipated needs of the beneficiaries. There are advantages and disadvantages of a will and trust that must be applied to your situation before you can make a well-informed decision. Both types of estate planning mechanisms have distinct differences in regards to how an estate is handled after death. Some people prefer to create both a will and a trust to effectively arrange their estate planning affairs.

If your estate is large or complicated, it is advisable to consult a good estate-planning attorney to take full advantage of various options.

While securing the family's future is important for all, there is no standard plan to achieve it. There are several strategies to choose from to secure your family's financial future. The right strategy for you will depend on your unique personal circumstances. Remember, what is best for your friend might not make the most sense for you.

Many people wrongly assume that estate planning is for the rich, but that is not true. The truth is that all people can benefit from estate planning. It is particularly important for the people who are rich in relationships. The people who really care for their family and friends.

6. The Matters of Money: Making Sense of Your Money Sense

It is a good idea to step back and take a look at how your psychology contributes to your wealth creation endeavors. Making sense of your money sense is not just aimed at making more and more money. Rather, it is intended to put your thoughts about money in the right perspective so as to optimize your financial decisions. Understanding your money sense can help you fine-tune your moneymaking strategies and avoid the traps of irrational behavior and false beliefs that often come in the way of objective decision making which is crucial for success in money matters. That is why some notes of caution must be sounded before the urge to make money grows impassioned.

The great physicist Richard Feynman once said that the easiest person to fool is yourself. He further added that one has to be particularly careful to find out not only what is right about one's theories and beliefs but what could be wrong with them. If we all followed this maxim of skepticism in everyday life, we can overcome any form of negative conditioning and make positive changes in our lives. But we do not. We tend to stick with what we accept as true. We just believe things, and then make our world fit our perceptions. The world's best-known skeptic and critical thinker, Dr. Michael Shermer confirms that the human brain is a belief engine, and beliefs come first and explanations for beliefs follow. This somewhat irrational behavior of our brain can be counterproductive to our financial objectives.

In our wealth creation endeavors, we are likely to encounter some barriers, which can significantly impact our moneymaking potential. We may or may not be consciously aware of these psychological barriers and their potential to get in the way of our moneymaking plans. Surprisingly, we are responsible for erecting these barriers. We often unintentionally fritter away our chances of realizing our financial goals by becoming victims of irrational human behavior.

Human psychology plays a big role in our money matters. It affects our money sense, which influences how we take our financial decisions. Behavioral issues can compromise our financial future by clouding our rational thinking. We often fail to identify the potential behavioral traps since they are hardwired into our thinking process. The best way to mitigate the impact of them is to become familiar with them and then manage them optimally to win the wealth creation game. Here are some common psychological traps that often lead to wrong decisions in the matters of money.

The Status-Quo Trap

We like our comfort zones. We all prefer to live within our comfort zones in every part of our lives. When it comes to the matters of money, we all have grown up with certain beliefs and find it difficult to deal with any change. We find it hard to profit from the change that challenges our status quo. But to create wealth, it is important to question the status quo and challenge some beliefs to enjoy the benefits of a great money sense.

The Status Quo trap is an inherent part of our thinking, which is often biased towards the current situation. We often have a tendency not to make or accept any change. Our subconscious mind considers the status quo as the safe option. Generally, human beings are predisposed to perpetuating the status quo because our psyche tends to be self-protective and risk-aversive.

The Antidote - Never accept the status quo just because it is comfortable. To temper its impact on your decision-making, you should-
- Review the objectives of your decision
- Explore other alternatives and use them to put the status quo in the right perspective
- Evaluate how your objectives will be served by various alternatives including the status quo
- Avoid exaggerating the cost and consequences of choosing a new option instead of the status quo

- Choose the best option after careful consideration of all alternatives

The Anchoring Trap

Anchoring bias is our tendency to give a disproportionate weight to the first information we receive. Initial impressions, estimates or information can unduly influence our subsequent thoughts and judgments. Anchoring bias occurs because of the initial impact of the first information and our immediate reaction to it. Dr. Michael Shermer reveals in his book The Believing Brain, "We can't help believing...Once beliefs are formed, the brain begins to look for and find confirmatory evidence in support of those beliefs, which adds an emotional boost of further confidence in the beliefs and thereby accelerates the process of reinforcing them, and round and round the process goes in a positive feedback loop of belief confirmation."

While relying on past information or data can help us to predict future trends, it also tends to dilute our perception of other relevant factors. While we cannot avoid the influence of anchors, we can subdue their impact on our financial decisions.

The Antidote - To minimize the impact of the anchoring bias on your money matters, you should-
- Be ready to entertain new ideas and think about an issue from a range of different perspectives to widen your frame of reference
- Seek information that contradicts your view, not supports it
- Avoid anchoring your advisers
- Avoid becoming anchored by others' thoughts, think about the issue on your own before consulting others
- Be particularly careful about anchoring bias in negotiations

The Sunk Cost Trap

We tend to justify our past decisions, even when they are no longer valid. A sunk cost is a past investment of money or time that has very little relevance today. But it is usually foremost in our mind and often induces us to make wrong decisions. While we know that sunk cost is irrelevant to the current situation, we find it difficult to divorce the two. We tend to believe that an investment is worth what we paid for it. This trap makes us susceptible to compound our past errors when we stubbornly refuse to ignore sunk costs in the light of contrary evidence.

The Antidote - To make a determined effort to set aside any sunk costs whether financial or psychological that clouds your thinking, you should-
- Consider only current price and future outlook when evaluating investments
- Disregard price paid when selling assets due to pessimistic forecast
- Take views of others who were not involved in the earlier decision
- Be open to admit a past mistake to cut your losses
- Analyze and learn from wrong decisions to maximize your profits

The Confirming Evidence Trap

One of our biggest curses is our peculiar disposition that makes it irresistible to seek positive feedback from others. Very few people value contrary views. We tend to look for evidence or opinions that will support and justify our existing and preferred point of view. We usually place more weight on our own position or decisions than they deserve. Many studies have established that people generally give an excessive amount of value to confirmatory information, i.e., positive or supportive data. In the financial matters, it can be a costly mistake to ignore or undervalue the relevance of what contradicts our view.

The Antidote - To minimize the impact of the confirming evidence trap on your money matters, you should-
- Remember to adopt a rational mental attitude towards your financial decisions
- Try to explore contradictory information and analyze it with an open mind
- Seek an independent opinion that constructively challenges your existing and preferred point of view

- Impartially analyze all aspects of the issue

The Herd Mentality Trap

Animals including social animals like human beings have an innate predisposition to follow the crowd. And many people prefer to follow the crowd in their financial transactions. They buy because others are buying and sell because others are selling. While many aspects of the herd mentality are beneficial, two irrational things can happen due to the herd mentality trap in the matters of money. People can become overly pessimistic when the market falls, and they can be too optimistic when the market rises. In financial matters, it is important to be aware of the pitfalls of herd mentality especially during periods of turbulence when people irrationally over react and take wrong decisions. When media exaggerate the reality of the current market situations during turbulent periods, gullible investors become influenced by the herd's emotional stampede, which causes them to unreasonably react and make wrong choices.

The Antidote - To free yourself from the 'herd mentality syndrome', you should-
- Avoid hot and 'too good' moneymaking ideas
- Always have a realistic view in your money matters
- Do not overindulge in money matters during the turbulent times
- Not panic unnecessarily. Have conviction in your long-term game plan
- Get your financial decisions ratified by a trusted friend who can challenge and question your decisions

The Overconfidence Trap

Research has confirmed that people usually overrate their abilities and knowledge. This is particularly true in areas outside of their expertise. The overconfidence trap is people's inclination to overestimate the accuracy of their decisions. Many people do not see the possibility of making wrong decisions and as such do not even try to evaluate the possibility of one. So, they do not prepare for risks. An overconfident mindset can really play havoc when it comes to the financial decisions. And it is really easy to fall into the overconfidence trap and very difficult g to come out of it.

The Antidote - To avoid falling into the overconfidence trap, you should-
- Try to know yourself and your abilities
- Get and respect feedback
- Objectively benchmark your decisions and allow for overconfidence discount i.e. margin of safety
- Seek a second opinion preferably from the domain expert in important money matters

The Mental Accounting Trap

We know money is fungible, yet we tend to value some dollars less than others and more readily waste them. We should realize that the money we earn or get from various sources is the same, and we should not categorize it into different mental accounts while spending or saving it.

Richard Thaller, who coined the term mental accounting, defines it as" the inclination to categorize and treat money differently, depending on where it comes from, where it is kept and how it is spent." Mental accounting explains why many people have a tendency to handle and value money and assets differently rather than rationally viewing every asset in identical dollar terms.

The Antidote - To avoid the pitfalls of mental accounting and use it to your advantage, you should-
- Always remember, money is fungible
- Imagine that all receipts are earned income
- Prefer to pay with cash instead of credit cards
- Analyze big purchases into its components
- Deposit 'found money' (e.g. bonus, tax refund, etc.) into your bank account

The Recency Bias

The recency bias is a psychological phenomenon that gives more importance to recent events than to older ones. It is a kind of mental myopia that prevent us to take a balanced view of things. In money matters, it can cause us to pay an excessive attention to the most recent events impacting market prices, while ignoring historical trends. While it is very challenging for the human brain to completely overcome the recency bias, it is important to avoid these mental mistakes and minimize the effects of the recency bias in our financial decisions.

The Antidote - To avoid the unintended consequences of the recency bias, you should-
- Be aware of the psychology behind it
- Periodically track historical data over a long period of time
- Regularly review long-term outlook and future trends
- Always have a long-term perspective. Think about the big picture in the long-term

The Mood and Mindset

The effect of mood on money decisions can be quite dramatic. Usually, people in bad mood make pessimistic decisions and people in good mood make more optimistic decisions. The emotions of fear and greed are typically strong after big losses and gains. It is not easy to rein in such emotions, which tempt us to make wrong choices. But it is crucial not to let our emotions dictate our actions.

Moreover, we tend to use heuristic simplification to control the complexity of information. Our brain filters some information and creates shortcuts while processing complex information to find a quick but not necessarily the optimal decision. Further, the cognitive dissonance also adversely affects our decisions and evaluations. It makes us susceptible to dismiss or downplay any information that contradicts our opinion. Understanding how our brain processes the information under these situations can help us to improve our ability to make better financial decisions.

The Antidote - To reduce the negative role of your brain on your money matters, you should-
- Rationally weigh the pros and cons of each alternative before making any important financial decision

- Minimize the role of emotions and mindset in your decisions by acknowledging them
- Avoid the primacy of emotions over reason
- Avoid narrow interpretations and over-simplifications in important money matters
- Check for unconscious reflexes and habits, and try to adjust to new situations and information

Understanding the above traps will not make you super rich, but it can help you to learn how to be watchful of your irrational behavior and, in turn, avoid mistakes that can decrease your wealth. It will help you to control your irrational biases with the clear thinking and make your financial decisions in a logical manner. It will also help you to manage your emotions and not be greedy when you should be fearful or fearful when you should be greedy.

To establish a rewarding relationship with money, it is not enough to have a great financial vision. You also need to steer clear of the psychological and emotional traps that ensnare so many people. What you do with your money should be dictated by your financial vision, and the human factors should not adversely influence your judgment.

Making sense of your money sense is all about understanding your money matters intelligently and taking your financial decisions in a rational manner keeping your and your family's interests in mind. In other words, it is about you, your family, your finances and your future. And it should be influenced by facts and figures, and not feelings and fictions. But then, getting hold of right and relevant information is increasingly becoming a challenge in this age of information overload. While it took a hundred years to double the information in the 19th century, now it is doubling every year. And it is a big challenge to sift the relevant information from the superfluous. Then again, your money sense guides you to deal with the information overload in a judicious manner.

We are not born with any inherent money sense. And we do not learn it in schools or colleges. We acquire it as part of our upbringing. And it is not that the rich parents inculcate a positive money sense in their children or the poor parents negatively influence the money sense of their children. The financial status of the family has little role to play. But our family's financial behavior plays a powerful role in shaping our attitudes towards money. And our social interactions continue to influence our money sense throughout our life.

Making sense of your money sense is a skill that can be learned. And it pays to invest in this skill. It can show you the shortcuts to your financial vision. Remember, this skill is responsible for the difference between people who thrive with money and those who do not.